DISCLAMIE AND TERMS OF USE AGREEMENT

The author and publisher have used their best efforts in preparing this book; the author and publisher make no representation or warranties with respect to the accuracy, applicability, fitness, or completeness of the contents of this book. The information contained in this masterpiece is strictly for educational purposes. Therefore, if you wish to apply ideas contained in this book, you are taking full responsibilities for your actions.

Every effort has been made to accurately represent this product and it potential, however, there is no guarantee that these materials. Examples in these materials are not to be interpreted as a promise or guarantee of anything. It is self-help using our product, ideas and techniques. Your level of improvement in attaining the results claimed in these materials depends on the time you devote to the program, since these factors differ according to individuals, we cannot guarantee your success or improvement level. Nor are we responsible for any of your actions. Many factors will be important in determine your actual results and no guarantees are made that you will achieve results similar to ours or anybody else's, in fact no guarantees are made that you will achieve any results from our ideas and techniques in our material.

The author and publisher disclaim any warranties (express or implied), merchantability, or fitness for any particular purpose. The author and publisher shall in no event be held liable to any party for any direct, indirect, punitive, special, incidental or other consequential damages arising directly or indirectly from any use of this material, which is provided "as is", and without warranties.

As always, the advice of a competent professional should be sought. The author and publisher do not warrant the performance, effectiveness or applicability of any sites or linked to in this book. All links are for information purposes only and are not warranted for content, accuracy or any other implied or explicit purposes.

United States of America, December, 2010.

2nd Edition Published By Jesse Imprints & Communication Services, January 3rd, 2012

The Creature From Egyptian Pyramid: The Revolution

By Ritchie Felix

ISBN-13: 978 1468171198

ISBN-10: 1468171194

Contact

Ritchie@before40.com, princefelixx@gmail.com

+2348039202454, +2348097888915

Product Manufactured From Eco-friendly Pulp/Paper

Cover Concept by Cover Creator

Interior Concept by Jesse Imprints & Communication Services

Printed In the United States of America

THE CREATURE FROM EGYPTIAN PYRAMID

"Unveiling the most guided secrets that the richest, strongest, and most influential people of the world want to keep secret for life"

RITCHIE FELIX

THE REVOLUTION:

Egypt is the defunct hub of Human civilization and remains a historic place of mankind till dates. The dominance of Egypt over the entire human history remains not just an act of God but also more of the act of historic figures that have visited the land. Revolution has trailed Egypt from the time of Joseph in the ancient Egyptian kingdom till time of massive conspiracy to subjugate the influence of the largest Arab Nation in the world. Egypt has huge income gap orchestrated by the deft Mubarak's control and average poor working class live on less than $2 per day. This economic condition was not just impoverishing; it was embarrassing as the government of the day resisted the slighted move for check and balances.

Partly, the Democratic model of the Western civilization anchored on the principle of Rule of Law as established in the Tenet of Democracy remained the main reason among many others that triggered the civic unrest that later metamorphosed into a full blown revolution. At first the Media could not establish the actual nature of the unrest either by error or by design as Mubarak shutdown the internet. Another prime factor that stood out as the cause of this revolution was the growing gap of inequality between the rich and the poor in the land. This is exactly my major interest here and my take away from the counter play of internal and external politics surrounding the entire event.

Average poor and working people were systematically suppressed from enjoying their vast contribution in growing the economy of the State. What do you expect from the people other than resorting to a violent revolution after a period of government apathy to lessen their sufferings? Their economic welfare was subjected to relatively unaccepted level of inhumanity and degradation. This model of economic inequality was originally invented right here in Egypt by the Hebrew boy Joseph under the water-tight supervision of the reigning Pharaoh of Egypt as recorded in the Holy Book Genesis chapter 47. This child of inequality, after being born, weaned and then christened in the West has been the greatest undoing of mankind in this ontological void - planet earth. The economic landmarks of the entire universe have not been the same again.

The rich people of the earth from Caribbean in the Bahamas to Cairo in Egypt and from the "New world" to Europe; and from Asian to Buckingham Palace in the UK have been in the business of growing the gap between the poor of the land the ultra rich either by error or by clear design. It is a normal thing for a group of people long neglected by the power of the State find choice in resorting to confront the system that has kept them insignificant, malnourished, unfulfilled and uncared for in a thunder bolt protest. But then, this would achieve so little as compared to when individuals decide to understudy the actual games or principles wield by the ultra rich that keep the poor in perpetual penury. Knowledge gathered from this level of awareness can be passed over to the posterity and this way the economic slavery which is the real game of the rich will be cleverly avoided.

What the Egyptian protesters have achieved from the violent revolution so far is a short-term solution to long-term challenge. Systemic wise, a standard and some level of decorum have been achieved, then, on a personal note the real principles and characteristic gimmickry of the rich that often retards the effort of the average person from getting above certain level of economic attainment on free and fair grounds have not been appropriated in place. I strongly feel that same way political independence in some oil rich African countries have not metamorphosed into financial independent of its citizenry is same way the revolution in Egypt will not translate into overnight economic buoyancy for the poor and average person in the land.

Individuals need to go back to the economic drawing board of the rich to glean out some necessary lessons to take away from this revolution, because sooner than now, a new conspiracy mill will begin to grind again, if it has not started already. What is holding the poor all over the world is not the activity of the government but the inactivity of the minds of the poor or the activity of the poor in the wrong direction. Wealth and economic fulfillment is a product of principles and formulae. Not a product of salary. It is profit, not savings. You cannot break into the zone of economic satisfaction wearing iron clad of servitude of a factory worker while you have the option of learning how to build just your own factory. It is the owner of the factory that set the limit of your economic satisfaction and the financial ceiling over your family head. It is so simple a lesson that even the mentally retarded can learn and become wise.

The Spirit of Tahrir Square
Call it the spirit of violence, protest, brotherhood in war, reclaiming back Egypt for the masses, and anything that goes for the interest of the people of Egypt. It is the spirit of self immolation, occupying the streets and iron clad resistance to "Mubarakism" or "Mubarakivian Rule". It is the spirit of 18 days that shook the world of Mubarak and that of selfish capitalist States all over the World. Armed with the Western script on peaceful way to toppling Dictators, the people of Egypt dismantled the security of the State as protesters invaded torture centers, occupied the streets of major cities and carried heavy write ups with different inscriptions.

The conveners of the resistance engaged the social networking online sites at inception to inspire young Egyptians to fight for their fundamental Human Right by taking to the streets and after the internet was blocked the people resorted to various media alternatives. This was just same way as protesters resorted to alternative media for communication in 1940s large scale revolution in Egypt. The spirit of Tahrir square brought together various opposition groups and guerrilla fighters to resist Mubarak maladministration side by side. For the first time, brothers fought for one interest to reclaim back their destiny. But did they actually succeeded is an important question of course? Keep your eyes on the watch, let's see how far this success can be sustained and transcended from generation to generation.

Occupy Wall Street

Occupy Wall Street was a total failure by all standard so long people fail to copy the games of the rich and engage the system by its own maverick economic matrix of the day. People occupied the streets from Asia to US, from Europe to the United Kingdom for months, but could not copy a veritable lesson from the ultra rich that owned most of the Corporation that suppressed the masses.

You may not need all the money in the world to do that, but you need to have the right knowledge in place and the gut to start out. This is the very mission of this book. For you to understand right knowledge from the wrong one, you need to first understand how the ultra rich wield their biggest victimization nest, how they go about it and where they lay their traps; and eventually who they use against the people and why. Like I did say earlier, this is the sole mission of this book – to help the average person fasttrack his income from peanut to significant desired figures that bring his entire dream to fulfillment just like the rich. Read and pass it on to a friend.

The Creature: Unveiling The Revolution

Table Content:

DEDICATION

This book is dedicated to Engr. Peter & Mrs. Rose Ojugo for their uncommon support and undying encouragement during my difficult times. Also, this book is dedicated to the poor, unemployed, those who lost fortune to the financial crisis and to young socio-political activists across the globe. Kudos!

SPECIAL THANKS:

Million thanks to my pretty Queen Christie Ritchie who provided me with the needed atmosphere, energy and synergy to take this masterpiece from raw manuscripts to resounding reality. Also, special thanks to Miss Joy Ritchie and Jesse Ritchie who helped in many ways to keep awake at Nights to complete this Book. You both are uncommon Genius. Bravo!

ACKNOWLEDGEMENT

This book is a derivative of creative intelligence and knowledge of team players located in the different parts of the globe. It is my honour to appreciate great minds whose works influenced my writing this masterpiece. Anthony Robson, Surveyor Jay Onwukwe- Author of Best Seller "Wealth Secrets you must know before 40" selling at Amazon.com, Robert Kiyosaki of Rich Dad Company- Author of New York Best selling series, Obike Ihechiluru- Author of National Best Seller: "Overcoming your life limitations" and host of others whose works have influenced me in several ways.

Special thanks to my Publisher who took this book from raw manuscript to reality. Now it is a great Sale!

WHY I WROTE THIS BOOK

If you ever do not want to be a victim of the radical changes in the marketplace of the 21st it is important you train like a victor. Only victors do not become victims anywhere in the time of change or crisis. What happened recently in 2007 in the global financial market will be an apology to what is yet to happen in the future and that is why this book is necessary to happen. It is neither a wikileak nor a book on financial advice; rather it is a necessary tool kit you will need to navigate through mortuaries of conspiracies to financial freedom.

Far back in 1997, every worker in the job market enjoyed high raises and large monthly paycheck, but after ten years in 2007, reality in the global finances left no words for enumeration. Many have lost their jobs and are re-entering into the hot chase for new jobs. Others are going back to the college to obtain an MBA certificate to track better paycheck or better job. The reality is that there are no jobs at the moment let alone getting one that can pay your ways out of debts. Who is even sure that tomorrow that a blip on the radar of technology will not engineer the worst change ever that could literarily wipe away your present job. This is not a prophecy of doom, nay, it is not it.

The mission of this book is very timely and strategic in bringing your way what it takes to stand tall in the facing of a dwarfing economy. It is a magical wand you need to navigate the oceans of challenges ahead in the nearest future that is inevitable to hit the World financial market such that it hadn't experience since the last Century. Hopefully, the central point of the global market will not hold together as people in different places will save themselves of the headache of using the conventional Money to invent something only acceptable in their own circle to serve as medium for exchange.

What do you think will happen when the monthly paycheck can no longer afford meal for two weeks because there are no foods enough to feed population explosion? The population size of the earth will soon hit above 7Billion people. Out of this number there are over 65% of the total populations that will live in less than a Dollar daily. Evolving technologies in information and communication technologies keep determining the strategies with which the governments and multinationals and other corporate bodies weave their policies that affects all. In the near future if not now companies will prefer computers or cybernetics or robots to work in the place of humans for the following reasons:

- Do need to be paid salary or make provision for Medicare for machines.
- Machine can work at unimaginable speed for 24hrs even without supervision.
- Accuracy will be a trademark of the day.
- Machine can even create other machine when programmed with right software.
- Machines can be operated just by one program under the supervision of just one person or none even from a mobile distance with a telecommuting device.
- Machines can handle Military commands and Mann aircraft to bomb enemy camps
- Turk machines can function with ultimate precision in any given assignment than humans in most cases.
- Etc

I do not want to bore you with information overload or cause you to nurse a kind of fear; rather I want to use this medium to call to order the minds of every reader to begin to think outside the box about possible Blues Oceans that can cause major lateral imbalance in the system to see millions out of their jobs a case scenario worst than now.

The good news here is that, those who know their stand in financial intelligence of this soon-to-be reality equation will supremely be on top their careers, fields and games. This book will help you develop that global competitiveness in both your career and ultimately in your finances. It will be wrong to depend on your company to expose you to the entire curriculum you need to achieve your personal and professional goals and objectives. Now, financial security is much more importance that mere job security. I wish you the best of experience as you read this masterpiece.

INTRODUCTION

What the Egyptian Prime Minister Joseph the Hebrew boy had out there on the shores of Egypt was a miracle, but what you have in your hand now is ORACLE! You do not need or look for a miracle if you have an ORACLE that creates one or more. The creature of Joseph instituted a world order that has transcended generation after generation to make the Rich-richer and the Poor-poorer, and keep evolving in its level of sophistication from National Ubiquity to global ambiguity. It is a creature of fate, octopus of deceit in the hands of the ambitious, and the very sophistication of the wisdom Age.

The principium of making money work for you is enshrine in the mancipium of good financial education anchored on self-will and driven by the blip on the radar of world- financial future. If you must rule your world with unlimited supply of money and roll in superlative success, there is need you understand the game of the Rich. Understand why, how and where they play this money fiddle and underline the reason why-while the rest of the world is dumped into financial crisis. The rich romances with unlimited abundance and makes love to their power points in hotel rooms across the globe.

This book will inspire you to attain creative intelligence, financial literacy and action-potency to make your financial dreams a reality in rarity. The pages drips with pearls of wisdom and juices of masterful artistic satire to crest your inventive and innovative genius loaded within the grail matter of your super-consciousness. It is the ultimate hype in the gallant fight against poverty embarked upon by the United Nations, World Bank, African Development Bank, UK DFID, USAID, and etcetera.

It is green with hope for the poor people across the globe, and serves as the much needed crystal ball to show the beholder the pathway out of financial strangulations of the immense global financial disaster. Albeit, it is ominous bad news to selfish wealthy and strongest people of the world. There is no room for compromise- you choose your side by the end of this masterpiece.

The flow of knowledge in the right interpretation and application of scriptural wisdom to the contemporary equation of the reality of 21st century remain phenomenal in this book. There is no dull moment from chapter one to the last chapter.

Ritchie Felix

CHAPTER ONE

"THE CYCLE OF CASH HEISTS"

The on set of Recession in 2007 marked the birth of another Era of Cash heist in the world history. The rich people are scaling up their Economy or rather business from mere survival in difficult Economy to the level of success and with the bailout cash, and then move into season of significance. Albeit, the poor moves from sheer survival in the face of this harsh economy to servitude; though with still elements of dignity, but by the end of this economic turmoil, the poor will be at the lowest ebb of poverty as slaves. This cycle has been around since the time of biblical patriarch Abraham. As at the time of Jacob with his family in Egypt, the scheme of the rich to keep the poor of the land poorer has assumed much more sophistication in both concepts and principles.

At the age of 30 years, Joseph, the Dreamer weaved this scheme in more apparent cash trunk bearing "Help for the people "but on the inside has: "Hold the people to ransom" After assuming the prime position of the Economic

Minister of Egypt during famine. Joseph cleverly stored food item in a pyramid order during the seven years of plenty, and waited for the arrival of the seven years of Economic crisis that massacred the entire world. All nations flew down to Egypt-the then hub of world civilization to get food. This included searching for menial jobs by foreign Nationals in Egypt.

The Holy bible recoded this worst scheme of the rich against the poor of the land in Gen. 47:11-27, here is the account.

"And Joseph placed his Father and his brethren, and gave them a possession in the land of Egypt, in the best of the land, in the land of Ramses, as Pharaoh had commanded. And Joseph nourished his father, and his brethren, and his entire father's household, with bread, according to their families. And there was no bread in all the land of; for the famine was very sore, so that the land of Egypt and all the land of Canaan fainted by reason of the famine. And Joseph gathered up all the money that was found in the land of Egypt, and in the land of Canaan, for the corn which they bought: and Joseph brought the money into Pharaoh's house. And when money failed in the land of Egypt and in the land of Canaan, all the Egyptians came with Joseph, and said; Give us bread: for why should we die in thy presence? For the money- failed. And Joseph said, <u>Give your cattle; and I will give you for your cattle, if money fail. And they brought their cattle unto Joseph: and Joseph gave them bread in Exchange for horses; and for the flocks, and for the cattle of the herds, and for the asses; and he fed them with bread for all their cattle for that year.</u> When that year was ended, they came unto him <u>the</u> second year, and said unto him; we will not hide it from my Lord, how that our money is spent, my Lord also hath our herds of cattle; there is not ought left in the right of my Lord, but our bodies, and Lands. Wherefore shall we die before thine eyes, both we and our lands, <u>buy us and our Land</u> for bread, and we and our land <u>will be servants unto pharaoh:</u> and <u>give us seed</u>, that we may live and not die, that the land be not desolate. And <u>Joseph bought all the Land of Egypt for Pharaoh;</u> for the Egyptians sold every man his field, because the famine prevailed over them; <u>so the land became pharaohs.</u>

Fundamental Lessons captured in the text above:

Joseph placed his father and brothers in the best part of the land, and gives them its possession.

<u>COMMENT</u>: In any adverse economic weather, the rich and their families are shielded from crisis no matter its

proportion. They usually employ the power of the state arts ands the legal framework provided in the National Constitution to acquire as much as they could. The same thing can be duplicated by any smart brain if the understanding of the Economic realities of the moment was achieved in the hay season of abundance. You can as well secure any part of the land if you have the knowledge, money, and the gut; you stay ahead of the games of the rich during Economic crisis.

Note, the people were not deterred from buying over the land from the original owners or from those it was given as possession. This people had their money in banks and other great assets to negotiate for a better future but they wasted time to decode the music tones of the on-coming depression. They paid dearly for this error of omission.

Joseph acted in accordance with Pharaoh's commandments and instruction.

COMMENTS- In the first place, Pharaoh happens to be the Head of security over the land, and the chief in command of Egypt. So why should he directly involved in this wicked scheme? It is only a question that you can answer for yourself. The rich has access to the power of the Land, has the Federal Reserve within his gamut and the law to back his moves always. It does not matter the style of governance involved, he can always carry out his subtle intentions if he so wish. Just same way as Pharaoh of Egypt was there in the ivory towers of the Land for himself and for his family; so several Captains of States across the globe are fastened over his people with his clever-woven arts to keep the poor masses in perpetual penury.

Every Nation on earth has the hands of Joseph the Dreamer within its frontline of power, but it is only the type of Pharaoh and scheme that will actually determine the extent to which the masses will participate in both governance and distribution of National cake. It is up for the Pharaoh to ask the Joseph of the land to duplicate his knowledge in the people.

He can decide to draw up wrong curriculum design loaded with stagnant schemes of work to keep the unsuspecting learners in the very dark of the actual realities that happens behind closed doors. Little wonder, was it ignorance or sheer greed, and avarice that made Pharaoh refused to enshrine a normal school system to enable the people build up their own pyramid scheme and be in money and naturally grow their own wealth. Pharaoh of Egypt blatantly neglected the issue of raising schools in his policy programs for his country. What a deceit?

In the Contemporary time, Pharaohs enshrine school system that feeds students with only what can easily and cheaply prepare them enough to go after salary jobs that on the long run will not result to financial security.

When the whole land was plummeted by famine the house of Joseph and that of Pharaoh fed sumptuously from the accrued fatness of the people's wealth.

COMMENT- At every time of battle for survival the rich scale up their meals tickets or menu and feeds luxuriously, at the expense of the poor. This is what I call leadership witch craft. It is happening before our eyes across the globe. The recent stock market crashes simply took away the money from the poor to the hands of the rich in the land. Investors lost their hard-earned savings, some lost everything accruing from their retirements, and others lost their homes, and other assets to the market dip. But make no mistakes to think otherwise about the company or conglomerates that are involved. They have simply taken away their money before the crash. How do I mean? The school Professor in your MBA classes will not tell you this. Even the stock broker agent will not tell this; neither will your banker tell you this. It is called the game of the rich to get richer and keep the poor poorer, at the bottom-line of poverty.

For instances, when George W. Bush government offered to bailout the dwindling Economy, it was the rich that were protected at the end of the day. Check up the statistics on the net and find out how the money was disbursed, and note who gets the fat, fatter and the fattest share. Who will pay for the bailout money? Of course the tax payers do pay for the bailout Largesse.

In Nigeria case scenario, the CBN Governor printed and disbursed the ₦400 Billion bailout (**As recorded by the Nigerian Bulletin website**: **nigerianbulletin.com/tag/lamido-sanusi by December, 07-12-2010)** all by himself. When confronted by the House of Assembly-he simply razzamatazz and straightway he was cleared by the legal frame work in both policy papers and the state art. The most minds bulging of all was the compulsive removal of some banks big wigs and direct appointment of successors in same stretch before the disbursement was done.

The Nigerian CBN Governor, – Mallam. Lamido Sanusi was applauded across the country, though there went out tears of agony in some quarters, of course many pains. Personally, I appreciated this sheer radicalism of revolutionary banker for his gut and sublimed poise to go on head long collision with some financial heavy weights and great players in the Economy. Yet all his antics and arts to fast-track the Economy on the right and healthy trajectory represented another hand of Joseph the Dreamer. Only time will tell the Pharaohs behind the entire scripts because the stage is still green with parades of arts and actors and actresses in this sub-Saharan region.

This gallant step of Mr. Sanusi uncovered the roll call of rich people who were making merchandize of the tax payers' money and that of unsuspecting savers in the affected banks. Some how the Economy of Nigeria is yet to recover from the derivative clogging the axles of banking progress in the face of global recession. His actions to this end- have been interpreted in various versions and quarters as either reform or sabotage of the Economy. You can pick reference from Tuesday Guardian Newspaper, December 1, 2009 – page 26 with the caption "CBN's REFORM" The summary of Nigerian case Scenario is that of wise Joseph working for Pharaoh or Pharaohs that only time will unravel.

Joseph gathered up all the money in the land and brought it to pharaoh.

COMMENT: - The Josephic kind of economic crisis is either deflation or inflation or both as the case may be. I will talk more about this later. Joseph did not force the money out of the hands of the people. He simply leveraged on the turn out of events of the day by creating a sort of cash flow diversion technique to corner the people money.

The unprepared generation actually bled so profusely from their wallets, savings and everything that stores value in it. It went up as usually, as everyday business and gradually built up to a crisis point. Before they could look up at the corner to discover what is on,   their money has vanished into the tiny air, but into Pharaoh's treasury. **It was late to ask who took my money.**

The same mill is grinding daily in several parts of the world right now. The unsuspecting masses are bleeding badly from every perceptible source of income. No Jack want to stop and ask on time what is happening to my pocket? What is wrong with me? What is wrong with my money? Instead, the people quest at the moment is to buy and buy. Invest money into this and into that, and at the same time consulting the wrong people for the right questions. What do you expect? They will get the right answers? For me, to lean on the shoulders of a banker or stock broker under the present double-standard is to take the greatest risk on the list. It is a suicide mission to embark upon. It is as good as getting injected with an old rusty needle by the hand of supposed medical expert. The banks are owned by the rich as well as the stocks, so you don't have to expect them out of business soon. The banker or stock agent will only supply you with pressures of sales pitch that will cause you to bleed the more from your pockets.

Watch closely at the game of monopoly that the rich play from time to time. Check up the history and become a good student with high I.Q. for literature review. The poor play same game but on the plastic board and never lift up the knowledge on that board to apply to real life situations. It is the failure to do this that makes the poor bleed financially continuously until he become poor and bankrupt of iota of hope.

You can beat the rich at their own games by creating your own pyramid scheme, nay, and network. Or in a higher word, you can create your own multiple sources of income because the secret code of the game is cash flows. The rich do not invest for capital gains during recession or depression. They approach investment with different mindset during persistent economic crisis. The mindset is to keep their money in a continuous motion, so they invest for the cash flow, and not for a long term dividend. Whereas the poor and ignorant people are tricked by financial advisors or stock brokers working for the rich to invest for the long term, that the economy is on its stride to hit boom again. And that it is wiser to invest now than any other time. This way they glean up the cash in the entire land into the hands of the rich. Do not forget your financial advisor or stock broker has nothing at stake, except his job if you fail to invest.

Somehow Joseph got paid handsomely from Pharaoh's treasury. He worked for his Employer and not for the interest of the people. <u>It is wise to know on time that every employer hands out a secret script to his employee which he must follow or adhere to whether good or bad, except he prefer to put his job on the line for another.</u> Read that passage above again, you will observe the flow of the scene logically in sequential order till verse number twenty five. It is not out of place to think that, the rich ploys their activities with the consent of the Ruler of the land. Or rather use the law as a shield to loot the treasury of the land. Well, life is a game of when you wake up to consciousness, how you wake up and where you wake up to this consciousness is a question for when you are prepared to wake up. Before the people wake up, Joseph had gathered all the money in the land into pharaoh treasury. You can only beat this level of smartness by becoming smart yourself. You have to wake up to the reality to the beatings of the global economic music of the day – to float your own network scheme with great product and create your own unending stream of cash flow. This way you beat the hands of Josephs and the heads of Pharaohs at work in your pockets. You cannot afford to stay and survive as a consumer all through life, you must produce either a tangible commodity or service or else you perish in the gulag of miserable poverty.

CHAPTER TWO

THE FALL OF MONEY & RISE OF DERIVATIVES

"And Joseph gathered up all that was found in the land of Egypt, and in the land of Canaan, for the corn which they bought; and Joseph brought the money into pharaoh's house. And <u>when money failed</u> in the land of Egypt, and in the land of Canaan, all the Egyptians came unto Joseph, and said; **<u>Give us bread:</u>** for why should we die in thy presence? <u>For money failed</u>" Gen 47:

The failure of money or currency to stand side by side with the value it represents marks the birth of inflation or hyper-inflation or stagflation in any society. It never happens anywhere by chance or as accident. There are always hands of Josephs or hands of Pharaohs responsible by reason of their own selfish activities. Could it have been part of Pharaoh's budget to gather the people money into his house and not into the government coffers? Or could this act be an oversight function of Federal Reserve or CBNs of the world? To take real money away from the people and offer to give them derivatives of it.

THE FALL OF USA DOLLAR MARKED THE BEGINNING OF WISDOM OF 21ST CENTURY:

- The USA Dollar lost value in the year 1971 when President Nixon severe gold from backing the currency. What is left for the people is history. As a global Reserve currency, other currencies of the world depended largely on its status. so as president Nixon severed life out of the mainstream of the world economy by removing the physical equivalent of gold in the vault, the centre of the world economy could not hold back again under pressures.

Since the global currency failed in the market place as in the time of Joseph in the then default Egypt, the world economy hit a bang across the globe and the reactions continued in chains from Nation to Nation, and now back to the origin. What do you expect? Your guess is as good as mine. The business of derivatives took over active system. Just like the Egyptians Dreamer –the Josephs of CBNs of the world including the almighty – Federal Reserve turned to quasi-money.

"And Joseph said, Give your cattle; and I will give you for your cattle, if money fail. And they brought their cattle unto Joseph; and Joseph gave them bread in exchange for horses; and for the flocks and for the cattle of the herds and for the asses; and he fed them with bread for all their cattle's for that year" Gen 47

It was when the USA Dollar crumbled in the market place that the Josephs of this world guiding our Federal Reserve and Central Banks smite the people with the ultra-wisdom of derivatives. It appeared to be a big bang theory and astute answer for the short term but not for the long term. Every bank started printing money from the thin air, and all became fed by instant riches but not for too long before the reality will hit the air. What stopped the Josephs of this world from seeking for other alternatives or ways to handle this crisis? The expertise to build a pyramid for each person was not lacking but the interest and willingness to help the poor masses was what was lacking.

In the first place, the pyramid was built by the effort of the people, though it was Joseph's master – blueprint, and pharaoh's commission. What was missing here was the president's ignorance either by omission or commission to empower Joseph to teach the people how to build their own pyramids. The school system is supposed to teach students how to set up their own pyramids and be in business for themselves. And not load them up with how to work hard for money to buy from the owners of pyramid.

* DERIVATIVES STINKS AND SWELLS WITH DEBTS

Derivatives stink when it assumes the size and terrific speed of flying bullets. I will talk more in details on what I call the BULLET COMPLEX-MATRIX in later pages. It is very hard to fathom the rate at which Central banks of the world across the globe create electronic values (money of course) and continue to do even greater businesses with it. Indirectly, quasi – electronic figures are backed up by debts as people keep borrowing the available cash in the banks to do business.

The debts swell at exponential progression in the developed world because there are not much paper currencies floating around, rather much more of credit cards and all that quasi stuffs. The rich of the land are having swell time junketing from Paris to Amsterdam in Holland, then to New York in London in spending Frenzy; while the poor are running helter-skelter to keep their jobs in order to service loans, mortgage and credit cards bills. At worst, the rich throw in towel over to the welfare for daily supply. What a negotiation? What a deceit? And what a faulty paradigm we run? Everyone is now a debtor to the state period!

* THE GSM BUG –THE BEGINNING OF MODERN DAY SLAVERY

The advent of Gsm took the entire world by rocket speed. For developing Nations, it is the beginning of another era of slavery that will last for generations. To get the license to operate a telecommunication service is as good as rubbing fifteen banks in Africa dry and clean.

The foreigners came into the Africa soil again with a near invisible mechanism by tag: "SIM Card" and mobile device to loot the treasury left over by –rich imperial masters. At first, it was difficult for African investors to come into the business so as to break up the power of monopoly of these foreigners with acclaimed message of development to take Africa to the rest of the world. Today, even the sons of Africans are there, yet the tariff charges for a minute call is quite astronomical compare to what obtains elsewhere in the world. What a help and plunder of people?

GAME OF MONPOLY AT ITS PEAK

The rich people in telecommunication sector whether white or black or red skinned have selected themselves again, and laid their cash flow pipelines this time not in the neighborhood but in the people pockets. By common sense in Nigeria for instance, there are about 10,000 (Ten thousand) bank branches and about 22,000 (Twenty two thousand) registered bank customers as the time of this write up. Nigeria has a population estimate of 150 million people, and about 75% of these populations are connected with the Gsm network. Just imagine about one Million Nigerians subscribed to MTN Treasury HUNT at ₦100.00 per Sms text that is for a day or per hour. That will give you whooping sum of 100 Million Naira, and only less than ten subscribers will be awarded prizes for winning each day. Just imagine how much this company made within the period this programme lasted. I leave you to research it out. This again is Joseph's hand and Pharaoh's voice.

Now, almost every telecommunication outfit in the country have one or two forms of creative cash flow schemes without giving back to the people in development package an equivalents of their profits quotients. Cash award is the greatest deceit of the game because there are other options on the walls of Nigerian development list. What happens to the power sector that is epileptic or seemingly dead completely in the country. What happen to the pothole-ridden roads, the antiquated school halls, missing school infrastructures, static standard of living, under-equipped hospitals, and the standard security system of the people? I leave these questions for the Pharaohs and Josephs of this multinationals to digest. Between August 5th, 2001 and 2010, the greatest import of this cash heist is kidnapping that is taking dead toll across the country. Much cannot be said about the achievements of these telecommunication outfits and multinationals in real terms. Mind my words: **in real terms**: I said.

It has boiled down as usual the poor making the rich richer and staying deeper in penury. I wish I could send the open letter of the Renaissance professionals which they sent to CBN Governor-Mallam Lamido SANUSI in Tuesday Guardian Newspaper of December, 1, 2009 to these GSM companies. **The rich have all ran down to the cities across the country that is safer while the poor berth in the hub of kidnappers. Only time will help the Josephs of this country to either save the face of this country before the international community or very soon enough- the kingpin of kidnappers will vie for presidency to occupy "ASOOROCK" What do you think?** You are entitled to your opinion – it is cheap and cost nothing to hold your mind.

*HORSES FOR BREAD "and Joseph gave them bread in exchange for horses; and for the flocks and for the cattle of the herds, and for the asses, and he fed them with bread for all their cattle for that year" Gen 47.

This is blank paradox! What a bargain? The drama in the scriptural passage above is the best way to define or explain away financial illiteracy. What is the relativity of a horse to bread? How many pieces of bread will equal the limb of a horse, let alone the full horse or even still, horses for just bread, this was one of the greatest cash heists in the history of man, since after creation under the heavens. The poor has always served best as fire wood with which the rich fuel his greed and satisfy him. The people gave away their horses, cattle in herds, and their asses to get bread from the rich people of the land. It is important to point out the figurative significance of the animals that are involved in this unhealthy transaction.

* Horses

* Herds of cattle

* Asses

Horses in the then world civilization was the highest level of investment of any average adult. It was used in ploughing the farm, used as a speed tool during war fare in the land; it was an equivalent of an aircraft today either commercial or private aircraft. It was used to travel far countries of the world in time of sudden disaster like war or natural upheavals. It was kind of merchant ships that navigates the high seas and makes so much wealth for the owner. The horses represented long-term investments with both transactional market value and capital gains at a long run. The importance and significance of horses cannot be over emphasized in the then world economic and socio-political realities respectively.

This is the same way things have been around from albinitio. The rich people of the land will prefer to rip off the poor of his widow's mite to become richer. In our contemporary world, it is essential to ask or draw the differences between the various investments portfolios like mutual funds, hedge funds and the 401 (k) retirement financial plans. Why does government encourages people to invest their hard earned resources in these portfolios? What is the hidden interest of the government behind these wise schemes that promises lots, but hardily delivers little? In 1974, the USA Government deliberately came up with the retirement plan that gave birth to 402 (k) portfolios, and at this, avoided the huge gratuity it would have paid retirees. So every one directly or indirectly plunged into the stock market unknowingly. Government took the people money away before their very eyes using the Josephic flips of magic.

Not until the stock market crashed that the people discovered that they have literally built a brick house in the tiny air. It was the handiwork of the creature from the Egyptian pyramid. The people money was swallowed before their eyes for lack of financial education.

HERDS OF CATTLES: The animals involved here were mostly used on daily basis on the farm land to generate cash flows. Some of them were dairy animals that produce milk and cheese; others were edible food and provided meat for the owners and also services as source of generating huge cash flows. The sheep skins were source of hides, leathers, cottons and clothing materials. These animals in their herds were given in exchange for just some loaves of bread for 365 days.

Pharaoh took away their money, cash flows and jobs away from them because the people were F-rated in the class of financial intelligence. Just same thing is happening to those who lack financial intelligence in the present world realities. Who took the jobs away? Who took your money and cash flows? Your answer is as good as none. The ultra rich in the land have many questions to answer for the current economic doldrums. But if you must stay focus and control the level at which your pocket is bleeding, then, you have to go beyond trading blames like every other person is doing right now to engage the rich skill for skill on their games. You need to sharpen your financial I.Q and build relevant skills in core areas of competence, and simply replay the script of this game to be in money.

With clear vision you can discern your future, and with right competencies grilled with cutting-edge knowledge that cannot be faulted in the marketplace, you can keep more money that you actually earn. This is called the universal law of attraction. Only 20% of the entire earth population operates on this dimension of economic reality. You do not need to be a nerd in the use of digital technology or a kind of political juggernaut to live from this ambience of reality. You just have to build the sagacity, consciousness, right charisma and character quotient to be the god of your own money.

"9" DON'TS THAT YOU MUST ADHERE TO AVOID PENURY:

1. Don't sell your horses for any reason no matter the pressure.

2. Don't exchange your horses below its current market price if at all you are going to sell it out.

3. Don't keep your horses stagnant, you have to engage it rightly to eke out living.

4. Don't trade or gamble with your herds of cattle, except you want to bleed to death prematurely. You need those cash flows badly to stay ahead of Pharaoh's derivatives.

5 Don't shy away from the Josephs of the land and the Pharaohs of the now, get closer and watch them, so that, you could interpret every move they make.

6 Don't hate the Josephs of the land because having them around fuels your ability to learn faster in the school of life financial education.

7 Don't kill your Pharaoh because, he alone has the vision or rather the dream of the land by destination. Instead, copy him in both skills and principles to escape financial insecurity. Every Pharaoh has the scripts with which the "Joseph" of the land functions.

8. Don't lose control over your pockets; watch what you are bringing into your balance sheet to ascertain its ultimate value status both in the short-term and in the long-term.

9. Don't eat up your cattle no matter the pressure.

THE ASSES "These animals can serve in the place of horses and in the place of cattle of sheep and rams. In other words, it is an average investment portfolio that has potentials to multiply gains for the owner depending on the market transaction involved. Investment portfolios that falls into this bracket, includes, commodities like gold, silver, oil and gas, platinum silver etc, and paper assets – like insurance, federal government bonds, blue chips stocks, annuities and royalties from intellectual properties.

As I was trying to conclude this chapter, I met a senior friend of mine on the way to my office. He has with him a black bag full of DVD discs, and I did not hesitate to ask what it was all about. He told me that, he has just done songs compilation in the studio and the sounds editing and mixing was concluded that morning. The DVDs are ready for sale he said with zest. I said to him, thank God you have just wake up though late but on the better side of himself. This senior fellow has been in the job market for years, but was never making ends meet. He served in various capacities on the corporate ladder of his then employers, yet poverty clustered around him like congregation of red pimples on the face. He struggled below the poverty line for years until he quit his job to delve into entrepreneurship. The tables turned around in his favour, he made some money enough to build his own house but could not leverage his business beyond his personal involvement. Moreover, he did lost good money when the market crashed. And now, he need cash flow daily to keep body and soul, and his family together. This was what inspired his debut in the music industry to earn cash flows daily from his personal sales, and royalties from his producers cum marketer.

I shared with him in precise words that rich people; usually earn or make money from this three category of income as follows:

Earned income

Passive income

Residual income

In conclusion, I told him to come to my office later so that I could help him to shield himself in the face of the on-going global scale economic conundrum.

Do not forget this: it is foolishness to sell away something of great value just to take care of a temporary challenge. You should rather think in terms of long term effect of its transactional value. You can really handle financial challenge with knowledge of leveraging on the opportunities annexed in it. Every melt-down in the history of any people usually come with wealth-down for some smart people somewhere. Open up your eyes now to behold the army of opportunities hanging around in your neighborhood and across the earth vast expansive space. The time of need is really the time of getting seed, not time to eat up seeds in your coffers. You can control the rate at which they leave your hand if at all necessity demand for them. And you must be intelligent enough to guide your seed because they are your money.

If the rate at which money leaves your hands exceeds the rate at which it enters, multiplies and leverages on the scarce resources in your hand, then, prepare for SLAVERY.

Ability to hold back money is never taught as a course in our school system, but it is knowledge you must learn to survive on the street. It is dangerous to spend money because others are spending at the same time. This is called *"crowd effect"*. The rich plan their spending and they are all receipted for proper account purpose. It is one of the many things that the rich carefully tugged away from our perception. Most often, what we spend money to buy ends up expending our chances of survival or moving from penury to plenty. While the rest of the world spends from our earnings, the rich spends from profits accruing from different business portfolios. Consequently, we pay twice for every apple we consume. This is a whole new shocking revelation entirely that will not be treated in this book.

CHAPTER THREE

EVOLUTION OF MODERN DAY SLAVERY

Modern day civilization started in Egypt so to attempt tracing the evolution of modern day slavery it is good to ones again recall back the scriptural text above again:

> "When that year was ended, they came unto him the second year and said unto him we will not hide it from my Lord, how that our money is spent; my Lord also hat h our herds of cattle, there is not ought left in the sight of my Lord, but our bodies, and our land wherefore shall we die before thine eyes, both we and our lands, buy us and our land for bread, and we and our land will be servants unto Pharaoh" Gen 47

Modern day civilization kicked off at the same period as modern day slavery. The creature formed by mental Wizardry of Joseph stood out like a colossus amidst the worst economic crunch of the then world. It was a man made mountain higher than any other natural mountain around that corner of the globe. The artistic dominated the

45

mental picture of whoever saw it because then, it was the first and only surviving wonders of the world.

The pyramid gave Pharaoh the strategic positioning to rule the default Civilization, and also gave the land economic power over every other Nation under the heavens. It was a creature of purpose that attracted the ends of the earth to Egypt, and the most potent tool ever invented by mortal to take another into captivity. It worked for Joseph and pharaoh same way it is working for the modern day Josephs and Pharaohs of our land.

Today, the pyramid of Joseph is built in the minds of unsuspecting many while dominating their psyche with working very hard for money. Consciously and cleverly, the students are not exposed to financial education all through their studies both in high school and college degree studies. The language of money is completely erased from the curriculum so that the students will live for pay checks all through their lifetime. It does not matter the name of the school or its location in the world-the system is just same in principles everywhere in the world. There is no school around that give the student access to financial education same way formal professional education is provided. This benefit scheme cuts across religious and cultures of any people on earth. It is what accounts for the vast chasm separating the poor and the rich apart. It is what determines who is advanced in technology and who is not. It is what is responsible for the under-development of several Nations of the world, because these poor Nations supply the workforce that fuels the engine of development of the developed Nations of the world. It is this scheme that kept several parts of the world berthing in incessant political turmoil and economic instability.

Ignorance is better defined as the mountain standing before many gifted souls that trapped them to a standstill in life. Ignorance is never an act of God, but an import of the wise Joseph and ambitious Pharaohs of the land to keep men in perpetual slavery no matter where they reside on the face of earth.

At times it is packaged and sent abroad via the market places of the world. Other times, it is transferred just same way as technological transfer happens. The scheme of Joseph to keep Pharaoh richer and the entire people in the land poorer is the worst weapon of mass destruction ever invented by man under the high heavens. It is a silent killer always around us today. That is why the rich do not go to war or battlefield, instead the poor man fight for him to protect his empire. And on the event of death the poor man family gets a ransom. **Warning**:

The Creature: Unveiling The Revolution

Check who is behind the ransom and make no mistakes to ascertain which institution, movement, empire or person you are actually fighting for. This is not a clear attempt to discourage anyone but it is worth knowing the real thing you are fighting for so that on the event of death –you die fulfilled.

Adolf Hitler, Napoleon, Alexander the Great, and the host of others had more than enough supply of the earth riches, so they mobilized men to fight for them in the disguised of fighting for their country and posterity. These men abandoned their families and conscience to gamble their lives away just for one man. It was unholy quest that saw many to their early grave. Men fought with their last pint of blood not for their land as purported by the words of these tyrants but, for the same purpose of securing the empire for one man. Some died by sword, others were consumed by the edges of thick forest, some were swallowed by pythons in heavy forest zones, and millions die by Natural disasters like the ice, cold and sea mishaps. There children were recruited into the army or field in their places, and wives turned into unholy mistresses to satisfy the sexual urge of those who could readily afford the fees, of course, most Josephs and Pharaohs gets the lion portion of this unholy affairs.

The Rebels:

The rebels are driven into heated war by the quest of one man, though unusually camouflaged as fighting for freedom of the land. The best way to get freedom is by learning the art of the State and by means of non-violent activism. Obviously, when such freedom is achieved at last, it is both empowering to the people and durable in operation. But, the other way round, few cabals uses the brains of many to build empire for themselves. Such empire plunk on the blood of men who died in war not even knowing the actual course they were fighting for.

The same Josephic scheme runs in the system of suicide bombers. The kingpins do not teach by example but by cunning ways and subtle means to incite young recruits to lay down their lives for the quest of one man or few cabals. One thing is sure here, for as the men die so their families because a man must be around in the home to model his children. Do you care what happen on your absence? What become of the kids left behind and who takes over your beautiful wife. While the entire Israel smolders under intense heat of battle with Joab the commander of King David army. The king himself was busy skyjacking the bell out of the war Uriah's Queen- who later became the mother of Solomon. Uriah died in the heat of the war because King

David wanted him dead by the hands of his enemies to save his face.

I wish this masterpiece gets into the hands of every man of war either in the field or out of the field. American people lost so much in the Vietnam War, and many brave soldiers lost their precious life not knowing what they actually fought for. Many homes automatically closed up forever and several families are yet to recover from the set back of this war. War in Liberia claimed millions of lives and properties but at the end, instead of peace after the demise of Samuel Doe the then president-the world watched two rival groups of rebels further plundered the economy and humanity in that country. What were the interests of the king pins of these two groups? Personal quest for gains or National gain? You already know the answer because it is history. Those that died in the war never knew the actual thing they fought for and laid down their precious life for. These ones again put on the portrait the picture of the creature from the Egyptians pyramid.

21st CENTURY SLAVERY:

The Joseph scheme in the 21st Century is a different joker altogether, but still same principle and concept at work behind the mark. The banking sectors of the economy are masters in this art, especially in the third world countries or developing Nations of the world. I have a banker friend who lost his job recently when his bank carried out down-sizing exercise to up-size profits for the chairman and directors of the bank. He told me that, he never saved a dime out of this work. He was employed and given car loan, and a set target of customers to bring into the bank. He did extremely well at that because naturally he has the charisma and the knack to convince people. He was promoted and offered millions of Naira as stocks of the bank, and his account was as well debited monthly to recover the amount offered him as capital which he never felt the raw currency because it was shares of the bank in the stock market.

When the stock market boomed between 1995 and 2005, my friend was in high Heavens. He even sold off some of his landed properties to invest in the stock market, and when the bubble crumble of the market came in early 2007; my friend was at the same time down-sized out of the banking market. His pay off was converted by the bank to take care of the credit facilities granted to him to buy stocks.

The gross net worth of his stocks in the market was nothing to write home about. He could not get another job as age was not much in his favour for bank Job. He tried his hands on few things but continued to lose in each attempt as if bound by a Shakespearean witch spell. It is simple, he did not have what it takes to survive and succeed in life outside the program tugged into him by the school curriculum.

He sold of   his car to feed and later packed away from town, that was my last to see him. Same ways many people not only in the banking sector-are enslaving their lives away on a job they do not have security. Even with job security the future is not guaranteed. My friend's experience taught me something very vital in my financial education. I did rather work for myself working for a multilevel marketing scheme than works for a bank.

This is because of the followings:

➢   The bank pays me salary which is fixed and limited in utility.

➢   MLM is not about a figure in the pay roll but an income system that keeps churning out residual income into my pockets.

➢   In the bank, I do not choose my exit, date of exit or how to exit the system anything can happen to exit me out of the system.

➢   MLM is a life time thing, but do not require a lifetime effort.

➢   When my friend was retrenched he left his platform with the bank, and the platform continued to create cash flows for the bank but the man that created it went down the drain.

➢   In MLM, one time effort pays you for a life time. Even on exit, your children continue to milk fortune from the platform you have created.

➢   The bank job will not give you chance to maximize other of your gifting, skills time and relationships, But MLM creates you abundant leisure, develop yourself and maximize life generally.

➢   The banking system takes after the Josephs creature in Egypt but the MLM is the opposite that empowers your pocket and body at same time.

➢   The banking system subjects you to training after training but geared towards increasing the profits for the owners, but not to guarantee financial security to you. Such trainings helps the owner make good merchandize out of your bag of skills, and when they have sift you dry and clean in most cases, the hammer of retrenchment will land on you.

➢   You are simply your own boss in MLMs but not in all MLMs because there are still Josephic in disguise. So take your time to study the TOS or policy before deciding to join any MLM. A bank job in the developing Nations of Africa is a form of modern day slavery. It is even worst in most developed Nations of the world because the "Joseph's scheme" assumes invisible status and works at terrific speed that normal person will hardly suspect a stitch of wickedness. Make no mistakes; the rich man scheme to undo the poor is in every industry and sectors of economy and polity of every Nations of the world. It is not exclusive preserve of the banking system.

HOW THE SCHEME OF SLAVERY IS SUSTAINED:

➢ High pay monthly checks

➢ On the job training to precondition the mind of employees to sign in for life, when such is not actually obtainable in most cases.

➢ Offer unsolicited credit facilities to worker to buy cars, houses and especially the company's stocks.

➢ Promises of Heavy retirement plan for workers when in actuality they do not control the forces at work in the marketplace.

➢ Quarterly promotions that come with pay check raises.

➢ Weekly allowances to enjoy your weekends.

➢ Build expensive rest rooms with eateries or restaurants attached. Every worker is usually encouraged to eat on credit to his fill, but the money will be deducted from source. You eat and sign the register. This is the simplest way to bore holes in people pocket and bleed them to death financially without them suspecting a foul play in the process.

➤   Create ultra-conducive working atmosphere to tune the minds of workers away from the real world realities around them. In some parts of the world, most workers live in the slums or quarters. The sight and feel of the exotic working place is the magic that fuels the worker's ego and indirectly programme them to commit life time to the serving their bosses.

➤   Create fun in the work place like party jamborees.

➤   Pay wardrobe allowance, hospital allowances and security allowances.

➤   Exotic holidays and picnic

➤   etc.

•   **REAL VICTIMS OF EVERY SLAVERY**

The real victims of slavery of are those taken into slavery by proxy against their will. These ones are the lawful captives of every slave master. The people said to Joseph buy us and our lands for bread" without a flash at the future. Of course, they forgot that neither Joseph nor Pharaoh was interested to spill their blood. But knowing the importance and significance of the deal – Joseph tied up the deal for Pharaoh. It became a law that the people and their lands become legal and exclusive possession of Pharaoh. They lived and worked to enrich Pharaoh and his household all the days of their life from generation to generation. This same picture is directly replicated in our world today.

- ## The First Slave Recruiting Agent:

Children born to slaves are by birth slaves themselves, and by the legal framework of the society are lawful captives of the slaves Masters. The parent of a "child-slave" usually starts out on time to prepare and focus the tender heart at serving the slave masters. That is why in our own world today, due to civilization, you often hear parents say to their child, go to school get good grades and secure good jobs, earn fat salary and invest in the stock market or Hedge funds. This is just some thing many parents did in the past centuries and continue to do even now. **Some Parents are the first slave recruiting agent that lives with the child and fights to model the child after the order of the paradigm of slavery.**

Those words sound very friendly and intelligent to ears, but it is the pass words to get prospective slaves engage in life time slavery. You can suspect those words if they had come from the lips of a stranger, but now your father or mother- who happens to be your first friend and role model is the one saying **"Go to school, get good grade and good certificate; cash on good job and invest in the stock market for the long term"** How could you have had suspected mayhem or evil of a kind in this pre-model advice of a friend and role model? This is why it is even more difficult to get people increasing their financial IQ.

What is Financial Intelligence?

Financial Intelligence is not one of the gifts of the Holy Spirit. Not an exclusive preserve of few who appears to have financial security, rather is intelligence gained from conscious financial education. Financial education is usually a form of education base upon the realities on ground in real time.

Nothing is wrong with going to acquire the conventional education to develop a choice career in the area of comparative advantage of national instinct. I passed through the lows and highs of the conventional education and I have to sharpen myself the more by taking up studies in applied scholastics education based on studies tool kits developed by Lord R. Hubbard. I took my time to appreciate the basics on the concept of: **"misunderstood word"** and **"word clearing techniques"**. But I never allowed my mind to be stolen from me by anyone no matter the conditions. What is wrong with Russians system of education on which our education here is based upon – is that students are programmed to take orders like soldiers, taught to avoid risks and do exactly what the principal or employer wants them to do. This is an indirect way to steal the minds of men and turn them to a kind of mortal cybernetic automated machine.

Therefore, **the conventional education system lacks merits in financial education of the students**. There are several other demerits of the system that I did point out in my book:

"Motivation for the Young People" It is a National best seller in 2007 and 2008 respectively. The high point of this piece is focus on "Emergence of New world order" that is fast changing the way things are done and reshaping the old conventions and tradition of believer in regard to school and wealth creation. As at the time that I wrote this chapter – the latest and upgraded edition is in the processing with the caption:"Motivational edge for young people" with the subtitle= "Unveiling critical principles to Rule your world" The book is very tight and I do hope every young person will find it to be interesting.

*Conclusion

It is impossible to accumulate wealth and preserve it over time without having a strong financial intelligence or education. The conventional or formal professional education only prepare students to be senior executive employees and rip them open for poverty to infest on them by the end of the day when the chips are down. Moreover, the economic merits of several theories of formal education are no match to the realities on ground at the moment on global scale. To stay glued to knobs of working for another to earn income is the easiest way to live in profound slavery.

CHAPTER FOUR

"MOULD YOUR OWN BREAD"

"Give us bread" to eat is not same as give us the recipe" to make our own bread, and not same as" teach us to bake our own bread". The givers hand is always on top and the receiver down because the two do not eke out living from same economic paradigm realities. The receiver's hand is always down because he never asks for the mould or for the recipe to moulds his own bread. The Josephs of this world are interested in sharing bread crumbs but never shares ideas on how to bake your own bread. The sharing place is the work places saturated with employees looking up the calendar to know when the next crumb will drop. The best way to define an employee is the one who waits on the master to drop the bread and rat-race after the crumb.

. It is a pity that more than 80% of the world population has been in this set up from the bible days of wise Joseph in Egypt.

Also from the time of Joseph till the present information Age, the world has never lack bread givers. It takes two to tango. Notwithstanding, it is unholy, and unequal tango because one is slowly going down six feet to be a thin history. Virtually all analysis of the world history revealed that in the time of difficult economic crisis bread-givers emerges into the stage with the worst razzamatazz to strip the bare flesh left on the poor of the land, and make them poorer than ever. It is not the situation on ground that makes the poor poorer but the unholy scheme of the rich makes them so. And the scheme never succeeds anytime in the history and anywhere in the history, except with Government interest. Umana Ponzi scheme in Nigeria failed because government did not have hands in it. Gold pay package scheme had crisis in early December, 2009 and this continue till the time of this write up because the Nigeria government was not directly involved. But the bailout quick fixes scheme of the central Bank of Nigeria-succeeded because there were cabals from the government behind it. The rich again in Nigeria were the ones actually saved by this bailout money. After the bailout what happened? Standard of living of the masses became worse and kidnapping business took over the centre stage.

"KIDNAPPING VERSUS BREAD BUSINESS"

While the rich in Nigeria are busy tossing breads in the air to tantalize the job seekers, of course the eaters of bread, angry young people whose destinies are battered and sold on the platter of bailout bullion took over the streets to rain venomous hail stones of terror on the people. Aba a hinterland city in the far east of Niger located in Abia State A.k.A God's own state turned into kidnapping capital of Africa.

In July, 2010, some Journalists visiting Abia State was reportedly kidnapped by these miscreants. This attracted the attention of both former and serving police Inspector Generals to God's own state. The Newspapers and media carried this unholy act in their pages, and the entire world watched on to see the climax of this drama. Kidnapping is not the best option to survive the government sponsored poverty scheme. I therefore condemn it with passion, but the truth of the matter at the end of the day is that too much has been stolen from the people via the government coffers in several disguised schemes like bailout money.

Again in U.S, Bernice Madoff Ponzi scheme made news in December 2008 and several media houses made fortune reporting this crack in its news dailies. It was obvious that Federal Government was not directly involved so same legal frame work that empowered him to float the scheme in the first place caught up with him. He pleaded guilty before the court on March 12, 2009, on eleven counts of criminal complaint for stealing over $65 Billion in investor money. But who should be hold responsible for impoverishing the people or the economy of U.S.A.? It is a question that only the Central Bank, nay, Federal Reserve and the rich of the land can answer.

"Bread" business is the exclusive business of the rich supported by the legal frames of the land, and even driven by its masks men. Yet, with good financial education, you can beat the rich at their game. For you to do this you need to have a propelling base or factor that motivates you to bake your own bread. This knowledge is very important if you must sustain your effort to bake your own bread. There is need you taken time to define your whys, how's and where's, etc. Lack of definite knowledge about the purpose of a thing is the beginning of its disaster, and the cheapest way to chicken out on destiny.

*<u>THE BREAD BECOMES POISON</u>:

Whatever you eat- eats you up too. The Egyptians in the scriptural verses mentioned earlier in the precious chapter cried to Joseph for bread. The wise one of Egyptian Ponzi scheme had expected this cry because the ultimate goal of this impoverishment design is to take the people into cheap slavery with their conscience red alert. This same thing; is

Is still happening around us today. It comes in various shapes, forms, packages, and nomenclature to get unsuspecting eaters sells themselves and next generations cheap into the hands of the taskmasters. <u>It will take long time before they discover that, it was bread that actually ate them up and not the other way round</u>. Then, it will be too late to make necessary adjustment to re-start life afresh. It is a sad allegory to say here, that many people are busy eating bread and romancing with their power point presentation in board rooms working for pharaohs and Josephs of this world without taking a second look at what is eating them up in the long run.

Sweet bread is often a sweet poison in disguise. Not all poison is meant to kill the victim instantly, sweeter ones kills gradually, but surely it kills the victim at the prime of his life. Fat checks, hype housing employee schemes or allowances, tantalizing social security for employees, over-size salary schemes and great vacations schemes are all programmed sweet poison of Josephs of this world. Except you add proper financial education to yourself-all these poisons will mess you up later in the near future. It will set you up, tear you up and spread you down in regrets, in sickness and probably send you to your early grave. The day you are retrenched, retired or down-sized out of the system is the day you get to know how much of this poison you have swallowed while throwing caution into the empty air.

When the chips are down, the fat pay check will cease coming, the official air is removed, you quit the staff quarters, all the allowances terminated, then the real man is reduced to his mortal size, but cleverly shaven of his dreadlocks of security as biblical Sampson. At this, your eyes will pop open to behold the ultimate sweet poison as the biggest game, nay, gamble; of fate that just destroyed you literarily without a tip of alert or alarm.

Naturally, it is difficult to discourage anyone eating up sweet poisons because of its instant gratification in the short-run. Even, personally, I make no haste to stop people from ingesting this capsules, but I am against taking it for a long time without switching over to an own thing, business or investment that can deliver financial security into your hands. Earn fat paychecks but don't chicken it into the hands of those working for the Josephs or Pharaohs of this world in the name of investment or diversification of investment portfolio. Joseph surely gathers everything back to Pharaoh's coffers and you may run into financial crisis.

When the stock market began to crash in the early 2007, more people were driven by the Josephs of the stock Market –that serves the owners as financial expert or advisers to invest more into the toxic assets with hope of reaping great capital gain in the long run. But today, the realities of the market at the moment left no place for just a word. The savers money, retirement financial plan tied on these stocks, and others has being gathered up back into the vaults of Pharaohs of this world. It is a double standard and cards well played just to keep the chicks in tight cage while the eagles roam the earth axis.

*SMART WAY TO DE-POISON YOURSELF

The smartest way to de-poison your system of Josephs and Pharaohs bread is not to stop eating and starve to death naturally, rather float your own bakery and bake breads for yourself. With the right recipe you can bake the best of bread around your corner of the globe. The most important thing is that you have gained freedom at last, not job security.

It is important you discover the Joseph recipe before you ever set out for adventure into the world of destiny. This is why I did say; you may not stop out rightly from eating Joseph breads. Having understood the nature of Joseph bread, you have to go beyond that frame of knowledge to uncover the various condiments that makes it sweet to the mouth of the eater, ticks in market places and sustained in quality and supply. Next draw up a plan for your exit, budget money for your business idea, get to know where and how to find bread eaters; and locate a market niche that you can cover considering your peculiar comparative advantages.

In the early 2000, I worked with Peter Franklin Secondary School as science teacher, and later switched over to lecture part time in polytechnic at the weekends. I discovered my presence and commitment to my assignments in the classroom gradually began to make news in the town. Soon the good news spread abroad-all the schools around lost more than 40% of their students to Peter Franklin secondary school. The management embarked on serious building projects but nothing was done to the golden goose that lays the golden egg. One day in 2002, I wrote the management for a raise in my pay checks which they turned down with all pleasure. I put in my resignation and walked away to consider life again.

The management had told me that I will soon be back, to beg for this job the day I resigned. Actually, it was not easy to survive without a pay check in view and without a job on hand. I tried to run some private lessons and coaching classes for some group of people in my church but still things were getting even worse, and out of hand. I did lost weight and become pale and hopeless. I decided again to take up a salary job, but was not prepared to stomach bitter insults and wickedness of the system or that of the marks-men that overseas them; so, I had to consider having my own thing. I baked my own bread by the end of the day, that is, I opened my own bakery to bake my bread. The name **"UNIQUE BRAIN ACADEMY"** became history in the town.

When I started, I had to teach the following subjects; general mathematics, further mathematics, physics and chemistry. Today, everything is now history. I have engaged people to handle the other subjects. I made sure that my teachers are well treated and have better pay-package in the community; and this idea paid off beyond my wildest imagination. They worked out their hearts and our students spread the news abroad. It is real great miracle; a sort of magic wand said a friend of mine: when in one swing scoop, the population exploded and bankers were everywhere scampering for my account. Soon I handed over other subjects to new teachers and faced administrative work squarely. Funning enough, I did employ some of my college mates to work for me. I now go by this respected name: "Principal", of course, I become a source of hope to many jobless graduates in town. I reclaimed back my destiny in my own hands.

My greatest profit in my new found venture is securing financial security rather than job security. Since then, I have ventured into many other things. I now can boast of financial freedom and abundant time to leisure away. This was not possible by my former engagement. The sweet poison was removed from my system, and my income system grows 24/7. This is reality!

You can do more than this, overcome the fear of attempt and launch into your dream to be the man in-charge of your personal finances.

Six ways to achieve your Dream in this wisdom Age:
You can not set out to pursue after what eyes or minds eyes have not_perceived_in the first place. There is need either a

physical or spiritual cause or object that should motivate you into action. The object constitutes your dream or target that you are focusing on to engage your scarce resources including money, time and energy. Here are six ways to achieve your dreams:

* DEFINE YOUR GOAL:

From the opening scriptural text in chapter one of these books, Pharaoh and Joseph had dreams each which informed their craft and ultimate resolved about the people of Egypt. It is your sole responsibility to define your vision or dream around your natural instincts and endowments. This dream or vision must be properly analyzed using both **SMART** and **SWOT** principles. That is: for

SMART:

S = **specific** – your goal must be **specific** and well defined.

M= your dream or vision must be **measurable**.

There must be a definite parameter either tangible or not to tell that you have reached your dream.

A= **Attainable** =set attainable goal or make your deal look real so, that it energizes you to give it the push necessary to bring it into manifestation.

R= **Reliable**= your dream must be real and reliable. That is to say it is something you can control in both input and outcome. It has to be something that you can easily ascertain at any given time.

T= **Time**= your goals or vision must have time lag from the beginning. Each step involved must be well followed considering time lag allotted to it.

FOR SWOT:

S= **Strength-** you must make sure you have a comparative advantage enough to pull your dream from point A to Z. It is wise you take inventory of your strength physically, spiritually, psychologically and other wise.

W = **WEAKNESS** = your dream must not revolve around your **Weakness**. It is important your vision majors on your area of strength and well guided away from your weakness/weak point.

O = **OPPORTUNITY** = There are always opportunities in every challenges; it is wise you utilize the opportunities around to give birth to your dream. See the opportunities in your dream, and de=emphasize lack or problems hanging around.

T = **THREAT** = Find what could be real threat to actualizing of your dream. Strategize to avoid or confront it when it shows up.

* WHITE-WASH IT ON PAPER= If your dream must be actualized with ease, there is need you put it on black and white. Do not forget written words have way to lift up from the paper to become life portrait picture in the mind of the dreamer.

* PLANNING & ANALYSIS OF DREAM/VISION

Planning is very important, and this is the place that separate dreamer from goal-getters. It is what account for the inability of many to take major and time, decision that can change their life for the better and best. You have to detail steps by step analysis on how to achieve your dream if possible develop a checklist to enable you stick to the plan.

* Engage others that have the relevant skills, gifts and talents to make your dream happen. But first, you have to make sure they have the interest to work with you, and must be available within the time duration of your dream or set goal.

* FUNDRAISING = You can raise money from friends, colleagues, the church and even go for a long-term loan which can be spread over into some period of fine –size repayment plan.

- **Implementation=** In 20/80 percent thumb rule, the 20% of the world entire population that constitute the richest among the whole "do" what the 80% of the world population had only imagined. It is "Action" that separates the Rich from the Poor. It is important you lift up your dream or vision from the blue-print into manifestation. You kick off with the implementation of your plan. To give room to procrastination is the sure way to kill your goal.

- **Checklist Your Performance** = Make it a point of obligation to check your performance or business productivity regularly. This will require you to have a definite accounting system where you record daily business or weekly business transaction. You have to develop a checklist to ascertain the state of the business regularly. This way you achieve desired results in your vision or business.

❖ **TAKE YOUR BREAD TO THE MARKET PLACE:** I made so much money selling my own stuff and other people stuffs than I ever made while working for my employers. I discovered quiet on time in my life that the difference between the rich in the land and the beggarly poor is SELLING. That is just the Billionaire code that every man must crack to become stingingly rich in life. **The Poor of the land are in the business of buying or**

bleeding. Money is the actual blood flowing in any man's life. Anytime you are spending, you are simply bleeding. If you lost so much blood, you may fall into comatose. Same way, if you spend so much, you fall into financial comatose- that is absolute financial anemia. Having a business that rolls out products or services or even both is not enough to result to cash flow. Your real business is SELLING what you give out to others to generate cash flow. If you spend more money that you generate through selling-you surely go down into the relegated waters of financial disaster. It is better selling more stuffs in every 24hrs than you spend buying in the market place. For you to sell effectively and efficiently there is need you explore the channels that the internet and traditional media provides. You can even engage experts to work for you at this point. Or you can register for few classes in e-commerce trading. You need to have blogging skill, website designing skill, graphics and affiliate marketing skill. Take your products to ebay.com, Amazon.com. Google, Yahoo, and other big marketing costumes on a global scale.

Vote much more time to create "buzz" around your brand on the internet. Learn how to take advantage of the sell opportunities in social networking forums and make your brand filters through software applications such as, Twitter,

Face book, Flicker, My space, blog sites, etc. Do not forget these software applications do not cost you a dime, rather save time.

CONCLUSION:

Internet is a strategy machine and can empower any person irrespective of location in the world. The internet superhighway is the biggest and speediest oven to bake your bread. The technology has literarily broken up the monopoly of the rich in this millennium. The millionaires of today do not need to own huge stocks, float many companies, and be in the government houses of the world. Or be in charge of the central banks of the world cum Federal Reserve. The millionaires of today only need to have specialized knowledge that has capacity potentials to create unending cash flow from the thin air. Additional Financial education will help sustain this wealth over time.

CHAPTER FIVE

"THE EVOLUTION OF TOXIC MONEY"

"The greatest cash heist under the Heavens is the introduction of the Toxic money, such that keep the holder under permanent debts all his lifetime on earth"
Ritchie Felix

"Joseph said to the people; Now that I have bought you and your land for Pharaoh, here is <u>SEED</u> for you. Plant crops in the land. Every time you harvest, give one fifth of the produce to Pharaoh". Gen 47:23-24.

<u>BAILOUT MONEY IS THE TOXIC MONEY:</u>

Nothing kills effectively and gradually like toxic money. It gives life in abundance to the giver and scoops abundant life away from the receiver. It is contaminated with deadly virus, that is, it is programmed in the order of matrix to keep the user in perpetual debt and economic impoverishment for as long as he continues existence. This was the exact status of the "<u>SEED</u>" Joseph gave to the impoverished Egyptians, of course, to the entire world that went to buy from Egypt during the famine. Every man and woman took this <u>SEED</u> home to their own country and the rest become his story.

Bailout money is never meant to empower the poor but the rich to enable them become very significant in the land. Anytime, the toxic money gets into the economic system of any people- there is ulterior motive behind it which is portrayed before the people. Little wonder, this government largesse find its way through backdoors of Central Bank into selected banks and outfits of the rich while the people purported to be the actual owners or targets of the bailout wait on the front door of these bank to access the facility.

You can guess what happen here. You get a credit facility from the bank, but pay more in the form of interest to the bank. Somehow, it will take the masses time to discover that this is government own kind of Ponzi scheme legally protected by the codes in the National Constitution. Although, it is exercise in futility. It is useless applying a short term solution to a long term problem.

What is the Economic status of U.S. Dollar-the global reserve currency after President W. Bush bailout exercise? What is the status of USA Economy after President Barrack Obama's bailout money? What is status of the global economy after the wide crusade of bailout exercises across the earth axes? Who gains and who is in pains? The money in every bank becomes toxic and that in every individual pockets become toxic too. China is a producing Nation and one of the fastest rising economics of the world, but I am afraid what becomes of China should United States Dollar remain the global reserve currency. USA is a buying Nation and China selling Nation-Just imagines the unholy romance of the two currencies in the long run. It is only time that will unveil the immensity of damage that is done to the global economy on a large scale.

♦ **WILDFIRE ECONOMIC BOOM**

One of the most significant attribute of toxic money is the instant or temporary wild economic boom. Right now, so many banks are offering credit facilities to their clients, the sale pitch of the media is heating up the tiny air. And all roads lead to various financial institutions to obtain soft or hard loans. Some workers are going back to school to do their MBAs, Microfinance Banks are selling off the toxic wastes to too many unsuspecting customers, and stocks market beams a ray of hope to tantalize new investors into the market .

Ask any average individual on the street about what he feels about the bailout money- you will be surprised at his reply. Ordinary, people without financial education fancy the bailout economy. They want government to print out more money. They fail to balance the equation with the rate of actual domestic productivity of the land.

This wildfire economic boom will not last for too long before the next phase of reality is set to shine in real life like the sun in the midst of heaven. It is important to note that the bailout money is a derivative of the future given to the people to eat up today. This is blank alteration of the cycle of nature. It is instant maturity from cradle hood by by-passing very essential processes that comes with gradual nurture. The toxic money will someday go back to the banks with the actual or real money as interests, then, the veil will be removed from so many eyes. This will be the worst cash heist of all time.

No economic growth is ever recorded whenever Gross National Expenses, GNE exceeds Gross Domestic Products, GDP. The fact that money is spreading like wild fire everywhere should not be mistaken for an economic growth or development. In actuality, what are growing exponentially in the economic equations at the moment are debts. We have to be wise to know that this is neither capital gain in the long run nor cash flow in the short run. There is need we match productivity with the activity of our financial policies. There is need this bailout money goes into the hands of those that fans the cold embers of our economy. The agricultural sector requires huge funding. There is need to fix our roads, hospital, power sector, create entrepreneurial schools and include financial education into our schools curricular designs. Much fund should be voted for student scholarships and National security respectively.

There is no sustained economic growth recorded anywhere by mere dishing out loads of money to the people just like that without handling fundamental issues of this magnitude. The deceit of bailout money is to rescue the system but not the people. The opening scriptural passage above dubbed it "SEED" and I like to it spell this in acronym as "SECURED EXECUTIVE EMPLOYER'S DIVIDENDS". And that is what actually it is on the long run. The Employers of labour supposedly the rich people of the land attained significant financial security by the reason of this "SEED" of Joseph. Blank reality!

◆ **NOT ALL EMPLOYERS ARE SECURED:** Anybody who wishes and has the power and means can be employer of labour, but not all employers are secured during harsh economic crisis. So therefore, not all employers of labour actually received the bailout fund from the government. The ones that received it have strong links to those in power towers of the world. Albert Einstein submitted "Everything is relative to a frame of reference either static or in matter." By connection, all ex-government administrators and serving officers have strong links to the chosen outfits that did received the bailout largesse. It does not matter whether they are "exs" or incumbent officers- all things according Einstein are relative. They are the really gladiators in the land in that, they are the **"Secured Executive Employers"**.

All central banks of the world are purportedly owned by the system, but the question remain on the lips of many "who actually own the system". Is it the people? Then, Mallam Lamido Sanusi- CBN Governor of Nigeria is in error for not consulting the people before delving straight to print security bills to rescue the acclaimed ailing Banks. If the people own the system, the WHITE HOUSE needs to clarify the people on actual mandate of the Federal Reserve despite the presence of US Treasury and all that meager financial outfits. Do we actually need a Fed Reserve is the question? Do we really need a "SEED" to come out of recession? What becomes the plight of non-secured executive employers at the down-stream of our economy?

And what becomes the fate of the people at the end of this tunnel of darkness? There are just too many questions to be asked.

The world's ultra-rich people are among these secured executive employers whose interests are protected by the taxpayers' money. Wealth or money is the object of relativity in this case with the powers that be. Not politics as usual. That is why, your bank will prefer to doll out billions in loans to the ultra rich while waiting on you to brandish a better financial statement and professional business proposal. How can you manufacture a better bank statement when you are just starting? These banks pretend not to understand. It is only time will uncover this game of monopoly of the ultra rich of the land. But however, you still have a choice to either watch in frustration to be recruited cheaply into slavery or make a decision to match this game skill for skill and knowledge for knowledge. What you need to escape the on-going "SEED" rendezvous is to equip yourself with proper financial education.

♦ THE SEED OR THE PYRAMID?

The Egyptians and the entire world at Egypt then, could not ask, Joseph for an alternative to the "SEED", they accepted it with all pleasure not minding the generational consequences, and went into cheap slavery of Pharaoh with their unborn generations. The wise Joseph knew for sure that the target of the pyramid scheme, nay, cash heist was achieved, quickly and cleverly sealed the "SEED" Economy with its attendant conditions into law in the land. What a game of deceit!

"Give us seeds to plant" and **"teach us how to preserve seeds to last for years"** are two different things altogether. There is wide economics of differences at both extremes. The Planter of seeds earns his living by his constant effort while the preserver of seeds put in just one time effort to earn for a very long time or even for a life time. What the people needed badly to come out of financial crisis then at Egypt was the pyramid's knowledge that can be translated into pyramid economy. Not toxic money or its "SEED" as was given by Joseph.

It was not ignorance on the side of Joseph rather a clear game of the rich to keep the poor of the land poorer and stingingly poor. He sealed this unholy deal with Pharaoh's signature which was supposed to protect the interests of the people. **Till this day, the signatures of the Josephs and Pharaohs of this world have done more harm than good to the people of the world.** Whatever WHITE HOUSE signs into law either place more value on the people or takes away value from them. It is either improving on the standard of living of the populace or impoverishing their standard of living. The President's derivatives either empower the social security, medic care and security of the land or it undermines it. What is important here is that, for every action or inaction there is equal but opposite reactions. "Every thing is quiet relative".

The "<u>SEED</u>" economy is a clever set up by the rich of the world to crash-land the poor in something more deadly than poverty. Only time will reveal how far we are closer to this reality. It was supposed to be a bond of freedom in it's entirety but for selfish aggrandizement of the financial juggernauts working with our Presidency- it is rather a bond of slavery.

♦ **THE BIRTH OF TWO WORLD REALITIES**

If the current recession continues, it definitely delivers two premature babies to the world. <u>One</u>: **a world of seed planters** and the <u>other</u> – **a world of extreme seed preservers**. Already, the chapter one has established that the rich exploits financial crisis and government bailout to move from success to significant success, while the poor move from just poverty to something worse than miserable poverty. I think the best adjective suitable here is slavery.

Poor Nations of the world today, supplies the gasoline to cook the food for the ultra rich Nations of the world. Poor Nations of the world keep seeking for aids to survive 'this' or 'that' but do not have the privilege to determine the conditions that comes with these 'aids.' Now if the people in this ultra rich Nations cry for help, then, those in the poor Nations will parachute to the outer space for God to hear their voices and probably perceive their agony. **Africa is the worst hit by the recession because of the level of under-development here before the advent of the global economic turmoil**. Most Africa Nations are consuming nations and have total income put together not greater than that of fifth richest person alive of the world.

Still, the governments of these Poor Nations are still dangling red carrots before their people. The self driven leaders of Africa still go for International Carrots "SEED" without considering the multiplier effect of its consequences. This way many on the Africa soil have been taken into slavery. This is what I dubbed "**Independent slavery**" a slave dressed in freedom apparel or cloaks. Only time will uncover the unholy romance of African Leadership with western power brokers. Something must have been traded behind closed doors that will be unmasked very soon should the tidal effect of acute recession set in. It could be anything that is traded before now and still on unnoticed. **Time is the real bomb!**

The "SEED" economy is set to empower the rich of the land, and keep them secure despite the level of insecurity around while the pyramid economy will even make the rich superlatively rich and rise to significance amidst the turmoil in the land. The "Seed" (Note, this seed is in small letters) will take the poor back to farming to work all the days of their life. Note this, the ultra rich uses the "SEED" to fuel the pyramids and keeps them in business of money farming in season and out of season. It is a world of two realities in both concept and structure and functions. Let's get it clearer here:

GROUP A – "SEED"

(Secured Executive Employers' Dividend)

The Rich:

- ❖ Owner owns pyramid
- ❖ Own a network
- ❖ Own an income system
- ❖ Has infinite income
- ❖ Has financial security
- ❖ Employer of labour
- ❖ Money works for him
- ❖ He is bailout on the event of financial crisis.
- ❖ Gets richer in the worst financial crisis
- ❖ Financial literacy is 90%
- ❖ Invest money for cash flow
- ❖ He sells either products or services

GROUP B – "Seed"

(Snr. Employee Extraordinarily Deployed)

<u>The Poor:</u>

- ❖ * Owner of farm
- ❖ * Owns work
- ❖ * Works for an amount
- ❖ * Has limited income
- ❖ * Do not have financial security

- ❖ * Employee working to earn money
- ❖ * He works hard for money
- ❖ * Pays for the bailout during financial crisis
- ❖ * Gets poorer or even get exterminated
- ❖ * Financial literacy is near zero
- ❖ * Invest for the long term
- ❖ * He is a consumer- an acute buyer

It is important to note that, same way Joseph of Egypt gave out "<u>seed</u>" to the poor of the land so that Pharaoh and his household will forever earn "**SEED**"; it is still same thing happening across the globe. You can only get empowered by the bailout money if you have enough financial literacy to leverage on the entire financial matrix at the moment.

Obviously, the Rich people world over are getting extraordinarily rich in the present financial holocaust while several employees are going back to school to get another degree or scale-up their career or even vie for a specialist course. But, all the poor man effort at working for the grid house is just to earn enough to relax in miserable poverty at the long run. This is not an attempt to discourage working, rather a wake up call to remind you that you need to work for yourself early enough in life to live the life of your dream. Salary does not make you rich but profit can.

Most advanced economics of the world are operating from **Group 'A'** Economic paradigm reality while most poor Nations operates from **Group B** Economic paradigm reality. It is a tale of two world realities. To beat the economy of Group B Economic paradigm reality you need to think out of the box and do things or approach issues about money from the opposite Group reality. This is what is difficult to do by many because of the faulty background or paradigm world reality that they are coming from. That everyone is going to school to register varying pedigree of certificates on their shelves does not suggest that they are all in their right economic reality. Watch closely, many have thrown financial education to the dust bin, and are battling the leviathans of '**red oceans**' to stay relevant to the job market.

CONCLUSION:-

Finally, it is important to note that, If you operate from **Group "A"** Economic reality you have the **real money** while if you are unfortunate to be in **Group B** economic paradigm reality. You have the **toxic money**. But you can decide to swap group if you have Financial Education enough to enable you come out with your own "**SEED**" and own your personal legitimate pyramid. This is within the realm of possibilities and that is the fundamental goal for writing this book. You can beat the curve of government Ponzi schemes and build your own "Autogenesis" (Self knowledge) and be in stinking money beyond the universal "dialogismos" (Imagination). Just imagine owning your pyramid to mint your **real cash** and square up with the ultra rich in the land. The next chapter tells you how.

CHAPTER SIX

HOUSE OF PYRAMID

"More than anything else, I believe it's our decisions, not the condition of our lives, that determines our destiny"

- Anthony Robbins

The Pyramid of Egypt is one of the World foremost Seven Wonders of the World built by the Hebrew boy-Joseph while serving as the Prime Minister of Egypt in the days of global economic crisis. In the then default Egypt. One pyramid sustained the entire world and did help many weathered through pangs of natural disaster as illustrated in the Pharaoh's dream. Since then, the Pyramid economy has been the sensation of the global economy. Somehow the ultra Rich in the land or across the world have made it their exclusive right.

MY GOAL HERE:

The many advantages of Pyramid Economic concept that utilizes matrix kind of program cannot be over emphasized. This book is not committed to detail every facts about the making, structural and functional configuration of Pyramid economy. The facts presented here is not exhaustive, but loaded enough to get your mind activated to log on to the path of destiny and be "Makarios" (blessed) with "Pleroma" (fullness) of grace. It is my expectation to see you come up to take your world by storm and refute the negative labels placed on you by reason of circumstances and events surrounding your life. This is my fundamental goal for writing this chapter to take you by hand and show you how to own a personal ATM, income grid or Pyramid, and ride on the wings of fortune in this wisdom Age.

PYRAMID= WEALTH CREATION: - It is not possible to fail with facts that have been tested over time, and that have proven potent in all conditions both negative and positive. Pyramid is a graphical representation of a system or network. It uses the Metcalf's principle in its actual operation. This is the singular reason the richest, strongest and most influential people of the world do not play with its economic prowess. Ordinarily, if just one single pyramid built by a slave boy could sustain the defunct Egypt in the defunct world civilization, then, it can do much for just one man. The soul that seat atop any pyramid anywhere in the world is always powerful in personality, high in ability, graceful in charisma and efficient in productivity. Such individual might not necessarily occupy White House in Washington, or Buckingham Palace in England, or even "Aso" Rock in Nigeria, and South African golden Palace, and all that; but where ever he is located, all things gravitate unto him. He is simply the god of his world and significant model of a type.

Why the buzz in the first place? He sits on top of the most powerful creature of all time- the creature from the Egyptian palace. The wealth creation machine of a sort that is multi-dimensional in operation, multi-dimensional in knowledge development, has multi-tasking ability, has ever-increasing speed and multi-inventive and innovative in relative to the future. The Pyramid of Joseph is equal to wealth creation device of the modern Age. It is a powerful and most durable tool for wealth creation. It is a strategic avatar ever invented by mortal man on the planet earth since the world began. It is still very much effective, efficient and efficacious in performance till this late.

PYRAMID IN A NEW WORLD ORDER: - In the recent times, information and communication technologies (ICTs) have become Key tools for productivity by both individuals and corporate entities. It has revolutionized how to see the world and how we live at the moment. This Phenomenal change has given birth to the contemporary e-commerce, e-government, and e-medicine, e-learning and all whole of the "es". This significant change has positioned the small, neglected, illiterates, less privileged in the society, the big money bags and others at relatively comparative advantage to other generations past in terms of wealth creation.

With cell phones, pager, fax machines, Apple I-Pods, Havron , I-Pad, Smart Cybernetics Machines, and lots of other portable computers, say one Expert; "The Physical locations are traditionally associated with work, leisure and similar pursuits are rapidly becoming meaningless". Computers and innovative communication technologies are bringing about a revolution that will make indeed, if not making now profound changes in all our known realities.

93

Today, Physical geographical boundaries have collapsed to pave way for the emerging world of virtual reality, and scaling up the global economy from analog speed to relatively more sophistication of digital nanoseconds. This is obviously beyond the speed of light. Old records are being broken down and new speed limits are being set every minute that passes by. This accounts in part, the cataclysmic crashes of both the walls of Wall Street economy and that of the stock market markets across the globe.

When last did you hit the GPO with your mail at hand? Email has taken over. These are all pointers that we are now in a new world order. You are not just a citizen of your country, but also, a global citizen of the world. Then you need to re-invent yourself to stay relevant to the emerging world of new realities. You need to build in global competitiveness in everything you do today, especially on the net. The super highway has drastically reduced inequalities among Nations and Nationals of the world. It is here to say good-bye to mediocrity and welcome to excellence. More brain less muscle is the trademark of this new world order. For the empires of today are build not with marbles and granites, but with brain, eyes on the screen and hands on tiny keys pads. It is "garbage in garbage out".

Now change is the newest speed limit, the entire universe has shrunk into a global house or neighborhood. At this, the pyramid of Joseph has been redefined in concept, structure and functional configuration. It is virtual, evolving and reduced to a digital bit. With smart brain and smart cybernetics you can evolve more pyramids of varying bit size in less than five minutes. Just think it, and then you have it with you. It is a blank reality of a House full of pyramids.

What Joseph had out there standing on Egyptian land was a miracle, but what you have with you or around you now is an **ORACLE** Period! It took him years, time, energy and millions of men to build; now you can create millions of pyramid in just a matter of 24hrs without breaking banks or breaking down your chromosomes. Welcome to the House of Pyramids!

▶ **NOW CAST THE DIE AND CRACK DOWN THE SPEED LIMIT WITH YOUR INVENTION: -** The rise and rise of novel technologies in "computer" and "communication

95

world" is bringing about a paradigm shift in the world of millionaires. The real phenomenon of the day is the reframed creature from the Egyptian land; **"THE INTERNET"** it is a technological clone of the Joseph pyramid that is the most leveraged tool of wealth creation across the globe. It comes with expanded content, context and ever-expanding world of realities. You have to know this simple arithmetic; your context plus your content bears your peculiar reality. check this:

► [Context + Content= Reality]

So therefore, to scale up your reality, all you need to do is to update or upgrade your content and context at a time, and then you log on to a new world of reality. It is important, you know that the two words here; **"conductor"** and "Doctor" come from same reality but the difference is in the letters; **"CON"**, which depict content. If a conductor of a train or luxurious vehicle on the street of African City changes the content of his mind with medical science, then, he dubs the tag "**Doctor**" period.

If you must cast the die and crack down the speed limit with your own noble and novel invention, then, you must be prepared to re-invent yourself in regard to the realities on ground.

Pyramid is now spiritual and has assumed a new speed order in exponential nanoseconds. The forces of "IT" and "ICTs" have made pyramid economy gone beyond the physical and moves with terrific ultra violent speed. What is the implication here? More millionaires hit the headline every 24hrs because speed limit is no more static in any field of human endevour, it is rather in a continuous state of flux. You can own your pyramid platform and mine gold or something more precious out of the thin air. Pyramid has gone borderless and then, civilization has gone beyond the borders of Egypt. It is near you and always lives with you. Supreme creature!

▶ **PYRAMID = NETWORK/SYSTEM: -** With the Internet platform, the ghost of inequality is banished to the void, if you are smart enough, you can create your own **network** or **system** that suppliers you with unlimited money and see yourself play chess game in Pretoria in South Africa, sleep 24hrs without stress in Paris hotel, ride in Roll Royce to Buckingham Palace to dine with the Queen, and play tennis with Obama in the White House in

Washington. The barricade of impossibility is eliminated, the walls of Berlin has fallen and grinded to grail ashes and the web is up and evolving into Ubiquitous to sophistication devoid of ambience ambiguity. The Ponzi schemes are over for you if you dare the tight cracks code-**KNOWLEDGE**. Age, Skin colour, economic status, political placement, religious affiliation and all that labels are no more barriers to accessing good life. What you need in actuality is **knowledge**. Make no mistake, not school knowledge or certificate stuff, and technological knowledge. Financial education is what you need to beat the game of the day. With cell phone, internet and specialized knowledge- you can become a significant player in the global economy. You owe yourself development and conscious self improvement. Bill Gates of Microsoft Corporation, Ophray Winfrey, Ted Tunner- Owner of CNN, Steve Jobs and Steve W. of Apple Computers, David Flo of Yahoo, Rupert Murdock .... etc are all owners of networks. **If you must stay out of work get a network**, and if you must sack your boss, first soak up financial education enough to have financial security. Information is power because of its inherent knowledge waiting to be dislodged and acted upon rightly and timely. You can fix the wrongs in the world and do away with the Loads of blames if you are passionate enough to make positive impact in your own corner of the globe. The Internet is here to say bye-bye to Joseph Egyptian model of pyramid that impoverished the people. Now, you can have your own thing and likewise others in vast expansive space of the universe. What we have now is a House of Pyramids.

▶ **CONCLUSION:** - It is not enough to have a network or have access to one; it is what you do with it that will culminate into either riches or poverty for you. If you only chat with friends online, write love texts and network with others across the globe without selling anything you still remain poor, or even miserable poor. It is good you come out with a blue print on how to harness the cash flow passing through the Internet daily. If you cannot create software, you can sell one through a registered network. If you cannot write a book, you can sell not only books but also much stuff as affiliate marketer online. You can pick up my National Bestseller. *"The Income Edge-Unveiling how to create money in difficult economic weather"*, to read more about how to create your own income multiple streams.

CHAPTER SEVEN

THE POWER OF PYRAMID ECONOMY

The most stable economic of scale across the globe is the Networking market business economy. This is same as what obtains in the true pyramid scheme with good products and services. A pyramid scheme without a product or services is a scam waiting to happen. It is same as Charles Ponzi Scheme or Bennie Madoff Ponzi Scheme. Good networking marketing business usually has solid investment foundation. It pays people from the outcome of the investment, and not the other way round. Everybody gets paid when the investment is due, and not when newcomers join the network.

Some Pyramid Schemes like GNLD, Gold Pay Package LTD, TASLY, etc combined investment, products and services together to deliver the expectations of members. I was once an active member of GNLD, Gold Pay Package and TASLY, It was awesome experience that I had, and will never forget in a hurry. I mentioned this few not to endorse them for you but for the purpose of emphasis. I became less involved in these networks when I received the call into the ministry. The network business operates on the economic power that goes with uncommon leverages that is infinite. Though, Gold Pay Package had a problem sometime between December 2009 and July, 2010, the company has been reframed, and back in business. I made quite good cash from these business opportunities. Within 9 months of joining Gold Pay Package, I not only made fortune for myself, I raised millionaires which ordinarily I could not do as employee.

I raised hundreds of groups of financial literate individuals who invested in real estate business, floated own companies, eateries, created own products and services. We were meeting Bi-weekly, and I always feature as the Speaker or Coach in all our seminars. Now, in the ministry, I am using the same formula to grow my church. If I could market products then, now I can take the gospel round the world using same experience.

Pyramid economy is the only business that drips with multiple income opportunities and leverages. As a member of networking marketing business, you can leverage on the power of the number to sell your own products like coaching DVD, Sales book, cosmetics, Softwares and others. There are Experts in various fields that you can pick one or two things from in the course of meeting without a fee.

♦ **BUSINESSES IN ONE BUSINESS**

For every kind of business that involves people, there is always more than one business derivatives involved. For instance, in Networking Marketing business, the following business derivatives are involved:

- Life Coaching
- Learning Opportunity
- Free or Fee consultancy
- Selling of ideas
- Selling of Home made clothing
- Partnership
- Joint Ventures
- Web Designs & Mgt
- Blogging Business
- Forum Marketing
- Article Marketing
- Book Publishing opportunities
- Driving School business

- etc.

The list is not exhaustive, as new people come on board to become part of the network; they come with not just their investment fund, but also with their profession, vocation and skills, including contacts. The Networking scheme fledges with personal contacts that are why in some part of the world it is referred to as grassroots business or home business.

If you are creative, intelligent, and smart to the letters, you can cash on these business derivatives in your peculiar networking marketing business to increase your earning pay checks. But make no mistakes, as Robert Kiyosaki always put it. "The best salary you can earn is learning while working" either for another or for yourself. Earning according to Robert K. is finite while learning is infinite. The most interesting part of any networking marketing business opportunity is learning. The opportunity to expand your mind, perspectives, enhances your charismatic quotient and professional prowess in Pyramid economy cannot be over-emphasized. It is real phenomenal and awesome experience you will never part with all through your lifetime on earth.

LIFE COACHING: - If you happen to lead a life coach by profession, you have the opportunity to getting more clients in networking marketing business meetings. Just dress nice, and move around with business card and carry yourself with an air of importance- introduce yourself to others and hand out your cards with disarming smile on your face. You will be surprise at the rate of growth of your clientele list. It is amazing to discover that the best place to get or meet prospective clients is in a meeting of this status. You do not need a protocol to access each individual in the meeting. There is this air of fraternity that exists in forum like this. There is bonding of purpose and affinity of minds here that you can leverage on to increase your cash flow.

♦ **LEARNING:** - The Networking marketing business meeting provides an equivalent of MBA business school platform to enable any smart mind to upgrade his financial education, and make the best use of every financial opportunity that shows up on his way. It was in meetings like this that I ditched the idea of working for another to gain my freedom. I discovered that I can make my ends-meet while leveraging on the platform of networking marketing business opportunity. In fact,

I quit my job at the apex of my career and till now, I have no regrets ever taking that life time decision.

The platform presents you with lots of learning opportunities from different team leaders, marketing gurus, and financial experts with good financial education portfolios. I learnt that I can maximize my leisure time to improve my other skills and subsequently give it cash potential to earn extra income without getting permanently employed. I wrote my first book then, and easily sold it all via this platform. It was in meetings like this, I discover that I could make extra bucks speaking in Seminars and public campaigns. This meeting made it possible for me to switch from Sciences to Arts. Today, I don't teach Physics rather talk about Money, financial education, investment, life coaching, selling, web designing and lots of others.

Learning becomes my greatest of obsession in life than any other thing. In the first decade of the Millennium, I started consulting for several multi-nationals, conglomerates and firms, and a regular speaker in many youth conferences across the globe. I get paid for my expertise, and in addition, I go home learning more things from my hosts. It is really a good life and awesome experience to mentor many to peak performances and classical attainments in their careers or pursuits. Do not forget, I cashed on this career while serving as a group trainer for a networking marketing business.

My attention was caught by the huge amount we were paying to guest speakers monthly in our general workshop training meetings. I decided to develop a career in this direction to expand my tool kits. Today, that decision has paid off beyond my wildest imagination. I have met and dined with political big wigs, money bags of varying pedigree and even Ambassadors of Nations on speaking engagement. You can learn just that much from no other place except on the network platform without having to exert pressure on your credit card.

♦ **FREE CONSULTANCY: -** At times, you need to exhaust your credit trying to pay off consultant fee. In networking marketing business meetings, you come face to face with consultants who might be part of the system, guess what? You seat down comfortably, sip your tea or chill soft drink and learn without measure an equivalent of Harvard

MBA business school curriculum design- topic on either business psychology or just course on selling dynamics

Again, you can decide to check up a good career in that direction. You stand to learn much better from this knowledge base group. This is great opportunity that exists in almost every networking-marketing business that is genuine; GM Motors is founded on a system and is sustained by the network of men with profound expertise. Likewise other coy, there is no way you take away this platform without having these business crashing to pieces. The Tele-communication business thrives on the power of network, and quiet often, some outfits grants fee credits to regular users of their network. MTN grant the night calls in some parts of the world, ZAIN Mobile now reframed do same but in a different package, and you can keep counting on millions of others doing same business.

♦ **SELLING OF BUSINESS IDEAS:-**The best place on earth to sell your business idea is in networking marketing business forum. You can easily get sponsorship or partnership you cannot ordinarily scoop from the street without exerting on your credit card. Most people that join networking platform have this kind of opportunity in mind ever before they joined. So it becomes easier to get your ideas across to people like this. You can as well sport legal assistance from group members in that field who will be willing to add value to your life.

Again, you can sell off such business idea if you are willing to do that. It will only take you proper packaging and presentation to get your prospective buyer convinced. Networking marketing business meetings is the best place people shops for cheap opportunities with great cash flow potentials.

- **SELL HOME-MADE CLOTHINGS:** - Most network meetings hold in neighborhoods or family houses, and this make it best opportunity to offer to sell home-made clothing's to guests and all in attendance in the training session. You can even sell on credit, and get paid from the source as a member of the system. Again, you can develop a list of regular subscribers and this is hype on your wallet.

  Apart from clothing's, you can sell just anything that is consume by people on regular basis ranging from perfumes, kitchen utensils, medicine, software's, DVDs, Computers, and etcetera.

♦ **PARTNERSHIP & JOINT VENTURE:** - It is important to know that people in network business have money as the prime purpose. You can share ideas about your project or business idea with the sole intension to get partners to move your project or business to the next level. Networking marketing business platforms have become achievers hub for those who get empowered by the system. The major assignment of these money bags is to raise up others into the status of significant achiever. Just imagine yourself aligning forces with these ones to create your world of great dreams, and live in unlimited supply of money. It will be really a world of wonders. It is a possibility and reality of several people you see around your streets. Obviously, you need not to commit crime to access riches from the cornucopia of earth wealth There is just so much for every one around. It is just that so many people around have eyes but do not really see things with it. There is a whole world of difference between looking and seeing.

♦ **WEB DESIGN & MGT**: - In this 21st Century, the password to wealth is the Web. The web is a hub of international network connecting all the earth together into a universal virtual neighborhood. Individuals and Corporate entities need the web to assume credibility, effectiveness and efficiency and speed of delivery of expectations and goals.

The web is a network of websites representing either individuals or companies. And as a web designer; the best place to scout for clients is in the Networking Marketing business meetings. While introducing yourself to other- offer to help them make presence online by way of owning a personal size website at a subsidized rate. Naturally, people tend to trust things of this nature to a friend, and expert that can be access with ease. Most professional Web Designers appears to be much more of a stranger than a brother you meet in a business meeting and also member of same place you belong. Think of surprise, because many will offer their web designing contract to you without shuffling an eyelid. The rest is history.

♦   **BLOGGING BUSINESS:** - These days blogging is gaining prominence and optimizes the search-engines ahead of websites. This has been proven severally over the various search engines on the web. So several online merchants and businesses are getting involved in blogging economy. The fact remains that there is need for more blogs and bloggers online than ever today. Taking up a career in this direction is a wise decision only if you know exactly where to generate or get clients. The Networking Marketing business meetings provides such a platform to meeting people who can subscribe for a proposal to have personal or business blogs.

Do not forget, one good turn deserves another —one satisfied client will recommend you to twenty others or more. You have to be honest in all your dealings and maintain that air of professionalism in and outside your office. It is advisable you attend such meeting with your laptop computer sporting your personal or business blog; and other previous work done by you. This is the other side of the business hinged on the networking marketing business opportunity.

♦ **FORUM MARKETING:** - The Information Age is not about product marketing but more about audience marketing. In our Network Meeting, we have achieved tremendous results marketing and teaching newcomers about forum marketing. It is simple and the most effective way of marketing products or services anywhere in the world. It work like this: get the man or woman that is connected to the forum or the head, follow up effectively until he or she sign up, then, relax and watch as others-Submit their endorsement with little or no effort on your part. It is really a magical wand in the world of marketing.

Note, Forum marketing is same as niche marketing. You need to take your time to learn the strong points or appeals of this forum, and enter them from this angle. You just be surprised at the results that will roll out before you.

You need to use the search engines to search out these forums, and then, study them one at a time. In most cases, you need to become an insider by signing up into some of the forums to know more about them. You do not need to be faster than your shadows, take one step at a time. Easy and gradualism are the secret codes of the game. Make sincere contribution in forum meetings, leave great thoughts on blog pages and write often on the walls of the site or on forum blogs to stamp your sincerity and professionalism. Next, get your acts and scripts in place waiting for the right time to strike and make your greatest kill. The rest obviously become stories.

♦ **ARTICLE MARKETING: -** Article Marketing is one of the fundamental ways to market your products and services in networking marketing business. You either write by yourself, or engage a ghost writer to write on your behalf with a back-link to your product or service site or blog. This way I have made so much for myself. Writes for Ezinearticles.com, Helium.Com, ArticleBase.com, ArticleRich.com, and lots of others. It is really a thrilling experience to see how this mark up articles sends back huge traffic to your site(s).

If you are not good at this, you can rely on article-writing software- it will cost you just some pretty penny. You can encourage visitors to your sites or blogs to write on desired topics about your products or services, this will enable your site optimize search engines, and even send more clients to your list. It is a true world of reality that several individual including corporate entities are enjoying at the moment.

♦ **BOOK PUBLISHING: -** So many people hardily discover the latent potentials loaded on their inside. It requires guts, passion and interest to get involve in the romance of pen and paper. But it is never impossibility for any healthy and sane individual. You can take up a career in the publication industry by way of taking up an online course in that industry.

As a money magnate networker, you can encourage others in same networking marketing business to write book in their area of specialty or profession or vocation. Encourage them to write their biography for posterity. Make them know how much you are going to get involved in the technical aspect of it, and you will be surprised at the number of clients you will secure just by that offer.

Again, you can encourage colleagues and associates to publish their photo files as picture book with a little write up to explain the circumstances around each pix. This way one can keep memory aglow for the future generation. It can make a good bed time story and serve as major source of inspiration - for others. This is an explored area in the budding knowledge economy of the 21st Century. I encourage you to cash on it immediately because it does not cost much to get desired results. Network meetings or training sessions is the right ground to get clients for publications.

♦ **CONCLUSION**

The school system bluntly keeps silent over this level of leverage that exists in the networking marketing business. This is what comes with legitimate pyramid scheme that has both products and services or one of the above. The level of contacts you get here will keep generating other contracts for you ad infinitum. If you offer great product or services- You will never be out of business because you keep counting success as the networking marketing business forum grows.

General Electric, General Motors, Microsoft, Dell Computers, Apple Computers, Ted Tunner CNN, and lots of others all have syndicates and distribution channels to keep their different networks alive. That is just same thing here. It is same principle in both concept and practice. Each of these businesses thrives on customers referrals, and usually makes space to accommodate everyone. The network is the fundamental business of the Rich and not the products or services that the entity offers. If you can duplicate this principle in your business, then, you surely hit your megabucks in no distant time. Just imagine what is the real product or service of FaceBook, Yahoo, Google and others. Their business though free, but the killing profits comes from the network of persons on these platforms. This is a fundamental secret that the Rich guide jealously to perpetuate their presence in the place of power and influence in the land.

I therefore encourage you, to shun that work that has kept you down for years with same result, and jump into a good networking marketing business opportunity to gain the potent power to unleash your innate wealth potentials to your world.

Chapter Eight

CHANGE YOUR MIND...CHANGE YOUR WORLD

As I reflected on the realities of the 21st century, I discovered that much have changed technological wise, socio-political wise and economic wise; but virtually nothing much have changed about the game of the Rich to keep the poor poorer, especially during economic crisis. This prompted me to go back to the Holy Scriptures to research how long such intelligent scheme of the Rich against the Poor has been around. To my humble amazement, I discovered that the Hebrew boy Joseph sold into slavery in Egypt was the precursor of this scheme. Genesis chapter Forth-seven beamed Search light enough to unravel the origin of this man-made enigma. The birth of this creature in Egypt accounts for the onset of modern day civilization which catalogued itself into a brand new world of realities full of possibilities driven by quest of men to become god to their world.

This unquenchable quest to attain supremacy gave birth to what we have today as university because men of great knowledge made disciples out of others who also

118

have strong passion for financial freedom, social security and socio-political relevance. Egypt literally became the hub of knowledge of the then world. Of course, the presence of Joseph and his mental import attracted the entire world to Egypt to get involve in buying and selling. Even, after the seven years of global economic disasters so many Nationals could not go back to their mother countries.

Some got employed to building pyramids for the Pharaoh of Egypt under the able supervision of Joseph. Others were employed in manufacturing and extractive industries, and others served in the distribution channels. The Nations of Israel along sojourned for a period of 430 years in Egypt from the onset of the seven years of economic disaster. Just imagine the population of souls in Egypt at that historic time, then, translates it to monetary equivalent in the form of revenue that accrued to the Pharaoh of Egypt periodically. It was obvious, the greatest network ever under the high heavens.

<u>Knowledge is the precursor of wealth, power and relevance, so the Rich in the land formulated the school system and its curriculum</u>. I guess they did put together whatever they want the poor to know. **It was the greatest knowledge heist** since creation-The poor were programmed to search for work to build strong and solid

networks for the Rich of the land. This way the clever scheme began to evolve into several models and dimensions of reality till date.

- ♦ **AFRICA IS PAYING THE HIGHEST PRICE IN THIS KNOWLEDGE HEIST:** - The contemporary Africa is paying dearly for this knowledge heist leading some parts of the continent into extinction when compared to the level of present day westernized development. The Imperial masters that colonized the continent; plundered the Spirit of ingenuity and brotherhood of typical African blood, raped the economy dry and clean before taking into captivity more than ten Nations of African into slavery. These men and women have their offspring living as Nationals of Foreign Nations and some in asylums not wanting to return back their motherland. Political independence in Africa has not yielded actual decolonization of the people mindset because the scripts of the Rich colonial task masters are still fresh running in the school system and in the Leadership machinery of every Africa Nation. Until you pay visit to Cape Town in South Africa and then visit the shanties where the poor live in wretched slums, also visit

Abuja in Nigeria and then Ogoni land in the Niger Delta the hub of crude petroleum, where the real owners of this crude gold are confined to penury. Nigerian case scenario of the poor is best described as miserable poverty. Somebody orchestrated these scripts of impoverishment and some Josephs are hired to perpetuate it. Go to Kenya and visit the horrible slums where the poor are living just to exist like wild animals in the game reserve. Visit Addis Ababa, and go beyond the territory to see the slums where humans are living in this 21st century, you will question why humans are competing with wild animals in thick jungle of vegetations same goes to almost all the African Nations. African leadership machines are yet to wake up from the stupor of imperialism.

African governments unalloyed adherence to monetary policy dictated more to pleasing the international financial system and investors than the well being of devastated population that voted them into power has further heightened the tension of global economic crisis on the African soil. There is greater circulation of toxic assets in this region than anywhere in the world for lack of basic financial education in the school system. The worst case in the Africa leadership is the presence of many Josephs and Pharaohs of a kind steering the State affairs for selfish aggrandizement. Who goes after the toxic loans abroad, and who signs the unbalanced trade pacts? These are two questions of importance that need no thinking to answer. The Trade distorting protectionist policies by the developed world have wrecked havoc on African agricultural output, driving prices to just around sustainability of the system. This is a direct import of the creature from the Egyptian pyramid of our present global economic buccaneers. The poor in this cleverly woven scheme just make enough to keep body and soul together while the very Rich swell their bank account in Geneva with unlimited supply of real money. The crack code of this game here is called SUSTAINABILITY.

Just imagine mere survival in the place where you can be success, and even significant is not a good thesis for impoverished people who can die in the process. I strongly believe that any one can survive with authentic facts if given adequate opportunity to try. You can change your world by writing your own scripts about money policies and create your own market to sell your wares. Where

<u>you are in the world is not important, the circumstances around you is not the actual determinant to measure how far you can go in life, and the level of your education, how much money that you can have in life.</u> The world is yet to produce a professor in fortune 500 group; you can dare to be the first.

<u>Your network is your biggest and strongest asset base in life. It is where you make most of your money, make yourself master of your creative knowledge and stamp your fact on the most leverage in life.</u> You can be the next creature with super-intelligence to rule your world and make history in the world of abundance.

Chapter Nine

SHAPE YOUR FUTURE

The future evolves and it can only be secured by revelation. There is this subtle belief by so many folks around the world that the future can only be secured by REVOLUTION. I strongly believe that this is arrant nonsense and not the sustainable way to live in this GREEN Economy of the 21st century. To shape one's future, you only need to do something different with your MIND. There is need to unlearn certain knowledge paradigm, re-integrate your latent energy in the direction of change and re-invent your financial intelligence. You cannot rise to financial stardom until you address the problem of your money problems in relative to your most esteemed financial intelligence. If you can secure your finance, then, you can shape your future without pains.

Financial Intelligence

All of us has money problem whether Rich or Poor. Each person's money problem is unique to challenge to an extent reflects the depth in him. It goes on to show whether you have the right knowledge to humiliate the problems of life or not. The money problems of the poor are the followings:

- Not having enough money
- Fear of closing corporations do to uprise in Global economic disaster
- Using credit to supplement money shortage
- The rising cost of living
- Paying more in taxes the more they make money
- Inflation

- Fear of emergencies
- Bad Financial advice
- Not enough retirement money

Money problems of the Rich are as follows:
- Having too much money
- Rising economic disasters in the society
- Needing to keep it safe and invested
- Not knowing whether people like them , or their money
- Needing Smarter Financial Advisors
- Raising spoiled kids
- Rising insecurity in the society
- Estate and inheritance planning
- Excessive government taxes

To have the right financial intelligence may mean to understand the dynamics behind money multiplication overtime in a sustainable pattern. It is not magic. It is both a science and art that can be learnt and practiced consciously till it becomes a sort of template registered deep within you that can be replete with aplomb ease. Making money is synonymous to bread baking. You can always bake bread any day and anywhere so long you have the recipe tattooed deep within the confines of your mind. That is exactly what it is! For what makes a baker is not the *'product'*, *'process'* and *'showcase' rather it is the requisite knowledge of bakery in his mind.*

Mike Zukerberg is one young person whose invention has changed the culture of the marketplace and that of the workplace across the world. He is a Dotcom entrepreneur with exceptional idea that is excellently differentiated in the budding financial empire of Web.2 Social Networking economy. FaceBook has over 400Million users worldwide as of January 2011. This is making FaceBook third most populated Nation on earth behind China and India if it were given physical landmark as a geo-political entity. The FaceBook Group headquartered in California is one of the rising Multibillionaire Silicon Valley Company in the 21t Century.

The company has a distinctive excellent mission goal to redefine the way people and institution relates in personal and professional grounds. At inception it was an all young people affairs, but just after three years of successful operation, the number of adult users not only increased but multiplied exponentially in progressive order. The company has successfully weathered through harsh competition from other social networking site and continues to tick gallantly in their unique business focus. The major product of the company is Knowledge and other services. In the super-industrial technological-driven era, new information transverses the earth's longitude and latitude in seconds, and fresh companies hit the superhighway in matter of minute. One of the major routes in the infosphere is the social media. In the future, the entire world will come to reckon with the social media as most innovative machinery of the 21t Century.

Develop People-Intensive Skill

The enterprise of tomorrow will be driven by People-Intensive skill, and no more by profit-generating skill. The profit of companies in the future will be the function of its consistent effort at effective engagement of the available People-Intensive-Skill workers overtime with right knowledge integration.

- Without knowledge you cannot reign in life

- It is knowledge that make you queue for change

- Knowledge is responsible for advancement in life in anything

- Nothing terminates sorrow like wisdom

- Knowledge deficiency makes men to suffers and live below their means

- Disgrace is absence of knowledge

- Not to be promoted in your job is because you lack the right wisdom

- Greatness responds to right knowledge

- People accepts you if you carry the right knowledge

- You do not rule in life by energy but by uncommon knowledge

- Lack of knowledge that can change your status in life is the cause of mental deficiency

- Poverty is the reward of people deficient of right knowledge

- Political marginalization is as a result of lack of knowledge. I mean no man is ever marginalize anywhere in the world because he carries uncommon insights about life. That you come from Nigeria or Bahamas is because you lack knowledge that is in high demand in the marketplace. If you have what the Buckingham Palace need at the moment, you gain automatic citizenship of the Empire.

- People lost their essence in their community when they are only better described as consumers. You can only add value in life if you create project and add up value in the marketplace.

- Apple Incorporation is product of knowledge

- Microsoft corporation is product of knowledge

- FaceBook is product of knowledge

- IBM is an import of Knowledge

- Coca Cola is a product of knowledge

- Hollywood is a product of knowledge

- CNN is an import of knowledge

- Knowledge is the capacity to decipher between the beneficiary and none beneficiary. It is the ability to arrive at the most profitable decision in life. It is the base of wealth creation around the world. Life is full of decisions and at every point in life – you will be confronted with confusion. And it is the ability to make a quality decision from the base of knowledge in your life that determines the quality of your outcomes in every circumstance, and your ultimate possession in life. Your position is a function of your knowledge base.

- The kind of spouse you marry is a reflection of knowledge resident within you. The kind of friends you keep is either adding value to you or weeding values away from you. You cannot carry a highly priced knowledge in the marketplace and be a character disaster. It is not possible. The ways you dress represent your core competency and reputation for the quality of knowledge resident within you.

- Dirtiness at times is associated with lack of Knowledge.

- Knowledge is the basis for profit in life.

- Knowledge makes you marry rightly with the future in mind.

- Knowledge is the pass code to unlock prison keys of life.

- People make decision but decision later in the long run make people. Knowledge is what you need to make good decision to be in strategic advantage in life. Knowledge is the ability to deal with the affairs of life. Knowledge is what you need to stay on top of the games of life and ahead of competitors in life. Knowledge is what distinguishes a man from his equals and make him stays way ahead of others in the marketplace of life.

- Knowledge is the capacity to solve problems and answer questions. It is those that have answers in life that will be in success, news and in unlimited money supply in life. Life is full of questions and you must solve the problems with sustainable solutions from the deep base of knowledge in life to be ahead.

- Etc

The mind operates two types of intelligence – Natural intelligence and Divine intelligence. Great creativity is encountered at the inspirational recess of the mind at the speed of telepathic impact of knowledge dilation within its intelligence. The mind intelligence in any context is depending on the way information is being processed by the two sides of brain activities. The speed of processing and articulation determines which part of the brain dominates over the other and deliver the prevailing reality of the mind.

Every object sound, touch and graphics can influence the reality of the mind at a particular time or physical condition; so likewise every word, tone and language. The mind always responds every data in a unique way depending on its prevailing reality enshrined by the side of the brain dominating over the other.

LEFT BRAIN ACTIVITY

- ❖ Good in mathematics and science
- ❖ Operates logic and its logarithms
- ❖ Responds to facts and details
- ❖ Builds of strategies from available data entered into the mind
- ❖ Interprets woods and languages with respect to semantics', figurative tones, and it's etymology
- ❖ Links pattern, create order and creates reality
- ❖ Articulate knowledge, creates knowledge and expands knowledge
- ❖ Safety consciousness, makes deductions from available data and generates the future or possible outcome
- ❖ Interprets reality of the relativity of present and past, etc

RIGHT BRAIN ACTIVITY

- ❖ Operates spatial manipulations
- ❖ Encourages risk-taking
- ❖ Driven by the "Big Picture"
- ❖ Forms belief system
- ❖ Adventure oriented
- ❖ Interprets reality from the relativity of the present and uncertainty of the future
- ❖ Thrives in inspirations at the emotive level of function
- ❖ It is the base of philosophy and religion
- ❖ Possibility oriented
- ❖ Connects to object at its functional level.
- ❖ Confidence, optimistic and resolute
- ❖ Acknowledges symbols and images forms symbols and images and engages it is creativity
- ❖ Imagination oriented
- ❖ Appreciates, depreciates and re-invents

Researches revealed that creativity is driven by the right brain activity. To expand one's mind requires re-inventing the "big picture", belief system and going the extra mile to explore the unlimited possibilities in the present considering the relevance of today's reality with the relative future.

The level of God's factor at work in an individual's life is the function of His relative knowledge resident with the mind of the individual. The same is with the type of leverages a man enjoys in his life time. It is difficult to separate creativity from the activity of the right brain. Until this side of the brain becomes superlatively activated into operation in our present context, it will be difficult to contend with the surprises or uncertainties of the super industrial revolution of the future. This future will thrive in instability and unpredictability as fundamental culture of the marketplace including workplace. The school block is yet to put up a match able curriculum for this blank reality.

I there implore you to work sincerely on the content of your mind, so that, your physical condition can be improved and influenced positively.

CHAPTER TEN
Spirit of Tahrir Square

The spirit of this historic square is the same spirit that produces great stars out of ordinary people. It is the spirit of uncommon leadership that inspires radical change in the believe system that has incapacitated ingenuity of men over the years. The spirit was not born in that square on that historic day, the Egyptians took their lives into their hands to challenge the uninspiring leadership of the Mubarak Junta; rather it was merely demonstrated. Likewise, the stars in us can be unleashed upon the society the day we make haste to challenge the status quo. It does not matter what we think about ourselves or about our future, so long we refuse to back up our thought with corresponding action, we continue to bath in acid of molestations of life limiting factors.

It was not the square that championed the change in Egypt, it was the spirit that each individual had working him or her that actually shook the World of Mubarak and that of the entire World at large. You can continue in penury, insignificance, poor job and in bad economic condition until you wake up in your sub consciousness to take responsibility of your life. Whatever the Mubaraks of this World do to you is because you consented to it, and you can change it anytime you are caught up by the Tahrir square spirit. The ultra rich cannot push all of us and at the same time show to us where to fall. It is a development crime if we allow the Conspiracy Mill of the ultra rich and corrupt leaders keep grinding our hopes into disadvantages, especially when we have army of ideas to beat them at this game. A real game is non-violent in nature and do not produce fatal experience in others. It must be positive and sustainable to be real great idea that can be duplicated overtime in other places.

The money game of the capitalist is fatal because they are driven by mostly profit and not in social responsibility as per se. In so many African countries, big time capitalists' institutions circumvent tax payment. Others sponsor social projects that lack intrinsic economic value in the long run. This is not just callous but a conspiracy to keep the poor and average individuals regardless of their talents and latent potentials in permanent penury.

In most developed Nations of the Western World, capitalists institutions can at least build universities, develop game village, create amusement park, construct and maintain roads, subsidized the cost of learning, and help in conflict resolution. In several developing nations of the world, it is paperwork here and there with barrage of white promises and lofty never-done intervention schemes. It is difficult to survive in challenging time as now that the global economy is witnessing recession either as individual or as a people whose hope is anchored on the mercy of corporate bureaucracy.

What is left for the average and poor people on the street is the right spirit to control the events happening around from affecting the stars in them. Stars in life are not men and women without challenges, but men and women who dare to hold their heads high in the sky amidst the paradox of deceit and sword of tyranny. Tough people are not baked in the times of peace but in the time of crisis. You owe yourself control how far whatever that is happening in your domain will affect you, and especially the star that is in you. let no man make you feel inferior about yourself or disbelief in your potential or doubt your special gifting.

You need the Tahrir spirit to keep moving in the face of draconian challenge. You need not engage in violent protest because you want a change by all means. The spirit is that of unity, comradeship, purpose and that of believe in own destiny. You need to keep going in the face of bad economic weather. If you lost your job, then, take it to mean suggestion to create your own job.

One useful idea engaged is more than a factory. It is an intellectual property on its own. Why should border myself about a job that is created by another when I can build my own company, create my own rules and parade my own mental wares on the stage created by me.

The spirit of Tahrir of square says it is *"enough of this"*, *"enough of that"* and *"enough of this nonsense"*. The rich can go on to pile their conspiracy game and create as many creatures as possible, because I have gotten my own protection. I have the idea, the star in me and the antics to beat them at their own game at the curve of competitiveness. I can save my world with my own invention. I can save others with my own brainchild. The presence of evil suggests to me the absence of the good. I can be the good for my family, community and for my country at large. It does not matter what somebody is doing selfishly or thinking about my existence. I am here to be the change that my World craves for. To me, that is the SPIRIT OF TAHRIR SQUARE!

We can fight Corruption, Poverty, Gender inequality, human trafficking, Prostitution, Famine, Terrorism, Dictatorship, illiteracy, Injustice, hard drugs addiction, crimes and Hiv-Aids side by side despite our religious affiliation. We are one people, breathing the same air and depend on same oxygen all through our lifetime on earth, and live on same planet-earth.

Whoever gets in our way want to defeat our purpose and undermines our truest value as human. We can co-exist with one another no matter our tribes, colour, religion, academic attainments, race, language and social background. This is exactly the typology of the spirit of the Tahrir Square. Let's wake up to this reality if we must build a sustainable future that we all can be proud to talk about before our posterity.

The Creature of the spirit of Tahrir Square

At the Tahrir Square, men and women went through the Process that saw them into the life *Showcase as Stars* for daring to challenge the status quo. It does not cost much take reach a decision, but it is usually expensive to execute the decision reached in the tough time. At the square, men and women who have criticize the Mubarak junta showed up to go through the cost of the process to establish their decision.

In real life case scenario, many people shy away from confronting the obstacles that have floored them permanently in disgrace. You may not go up in life if you cannot make up your mind to weather through the process of the Tahrir Square. It may be time consuming. It may be you need to prove your haters wrong by taking that decision that will rest argument in your favour. It may be fatal to even attempt and fail, so you have to take up decision not to fail in the first place. What separate the Stars from the rest of us is very tiny:

- Stars are smarter, they have higher IQs

- Stars are better problem solvers and more creative

- Stars are more ambitious; they have a "will to succeed".

- Stars are more outgoing; they get along well with people

- Stars are risk takers and maverick when necessary.

- Stars usually have publications, Patents and Awards

- Stars have clarity, competence and concentration

- Stars recognizes latent potentials and are restless people

- Stars are very hard and smart working people

- Stars talks and lives in the picture of the future in their minds.

- Stars are focus, unwavering, perseverance and solution-driven

In a Produce-or-perish economy of our present World realities, you do not need to applaud labour-intensiveness ahead of Knowledge-intensiveness. You need to develop the following three to be above limiting factors:

- 1. Clarity

- 2. Competence

- 3. Concentration

- One of the biggest problems of this century is that of an average person without a program, not ready to identify own process to get to the life showcase, because he or she lacks concentration.

- Something great that incubates stars cannot sit on you if you cannot sit down on purpose. The spirit of God cannot incubate on you for something extraordinary if you cannot sit down in His presence for too long a <u>Time.</u>

- You need to chisel out working strategies that can grant you the speed you need to both break into the place of Power and into the Palace of Purpose (Divine Purpose for your life).

- In the 21st century, stars are Brainpowered people.

- Stars are men & women who have decided to be restless and refused to settle for the handouts of status quo.

- They understand the prize to be won if one is willing enough to pay the price to go through the process.

- They are not ready to give up easily the conviction that they are star-materials despite life overwhelming limitations and realities respectively.

- They understand the deep psychological satisfaction that comes into play when the odds of life are overturn to fit into ultimate purpose of their being.. They understand that on the internal track of life you are competing with yourself to be the best you know you can be.

- They understand that whenever this is achieved, you would have gained mastery, attained fulfillment of your personal investment in Time and other Resources, gained the respect of your peers and contemporaries, defined your personality identity and declared yourself worthy before all eyes.

Comparing what happened at the Tahrir Square and what happened at the Pyramid of Joseph one can see from afar the efficacy of timely action anchored on the prevailing knowledge of the day.

Africa: Battles for the Future

Money is what makes the World to go round from East to West and South to North in season and out of season. Rosabeth Moss opined that *"You have no future until you add value and Create Projects"*. All over the world right now, there is a battle going on unspoken but raging in full glare of all. Nations are scampering to secure their feet firmly in the financial future of the global economy.

Advanced Nations are advancing their *technologies* and *crack-codes* for wealth creation in the future. China is hoping to join forces with partners abroad to leapfrog her Economy and champion the economic revolution of the future. Two attractive Markets are gradually opening across the longitudes of the universe; one in the African Continent and the others in the Asian Platform. There is a growing market in computer technology in Africa right now than ever. Only few players are in this market at the moment because of its peculiarity and height of insecurity in the region at the moment.

Strategic investment in Africa first requires major investment in security and second in the development of indigent manpower to reduce total overhead cost of operation. Engaging expatriates will rather inflame the total overhead cost of production, which will strangle the chances of survival in the face of stringent competition or economic bad weather. Nevertheless, the advantages of engaging expatriates cannot be over-emphasized. The chances of creating a sustainable base for growth and development is estimated to be 85% and above. Only few players are able to go against the odds to track their organization on this pitch of productivity.

Esther Dyson posited: *"owning the intellectual property is like owning land: You need to keep investing in it again and again to get a payoff, you can't simply sit back and collect rent"*. By implication, what companies require for profit or productivity is not just land but something more significance and rewarding if properly developed and gainfully deployed at work. In both 19th and 20th Century – Land played great role in determining the final LCM in the chain of production. It was a labour-intensive era not same as knowledge-intensive climate of the 21st Century.

Nations without the intellectual capacity to drive her economy will remain chained to antiquity and under-development of her natural economic potentials. Nations with so little landscape but have qualitative manpower or brainpower according to Brain Tracey will bask in multiplication of opportunities and leverages for uncommon growth and development of her economy.

Nation like Singapore advanced in Human Capital Development first ever before setting out to tap into the numerous opportunities that come with recent technological revolutions. Several Nations of the World gets supply of essential commodities from Singapore now and this is helping in the growth of the Country GDP while tracking down her dependence on importation. It is usually difficult to grow an individual economy less a Nation economy on external dependence.

Productivity seems to favour knowledge Workers in the present economic order ahead of traditional machine or manual workers. Ordinary individuals working for firms stand little chance to attain financial freedom working with just a set of default skill kit or certificate gotten on graduation from the University. One individual need loads of skill set to stay on top the game to secure a favourable financial Future.

Dot.Com bubbles at the end of the 20th Century saw multinationals scampering to get firm hold of the supply chain. EBay the internet service enabled new comers to come in the market and yet causes extra bubble at the end of the tunnel. After much experimentation – eBay remains a glorified B2B exchange service alternative that only grant Consumer the privilege to get the best of product or service of any brand or category anywhere in the world at real time at a cost-effective price. Moreover, further debut of other online exchange services saw the boom of infant industries and private entrepreneurs going home with mouth watering profits.

Knowledge in Equation of Money Creation:
The new currency in town is called information. It is precursor of the specialized knowledge that is required in money creation. Knowing about an idea is not enough to guarantee wealth creation in any field of Endeavour. Rather having an exceptional working knowledge about the *pros* and *cons* of it active engagement that guarantees money creation in abundance. Information is useless if it cannot deliver the immediate ends on engagement.
Evans Esar said; *"Hindsight is good, foresight is better, but second sight is the best of all"* The second sight is usually special knowledge that has the capacity for

proficiency, effectiveness and productivity. Several companies including; individual functions with half-baked knowledge that cannot stand the tinted competition of the marketplace.

Second market that is opening up at the moment is the rise of social media like FaceBook, MySpace, Flickr, Twitter, Skype, LinkedIn, and etcetera. Several companies using the internet platform to cut down on the size of their employment batch and upsized profits are kilometers away from loses. For instance, if FaceBook were to have a geographic landmark as a Nation it surely grows into the largest in the comet of Nations on earth in the next decade following its current stride of growth daily.

Four areas that requires strategic attention in every Nation across the poles of the universe includes:
1. Personal Development

2. Growth of GDP of National economy

3. Regional Development

4. Global participation

. **Personal Development**: In the information age or knowledge age the total Human Capital or rather Intellectual Capital of a Nation represents the actual asset of the Nation. It is an index that that surely vary the general equity of the economic system at any given time. Machines, Land, Precious Stones or Minerals including others and agricultural products now represents minors in the analysis or summation of the GDP of any Nation.

While several advanced economies are fast negotiating better future in the infosphere of the of the new age, many others, especially African Nations are busy hauling missiles and spraying bullets against their citizenry in stringent battle for leadership positions. What become the consequences at the end of the day? The poor masses pay for all the destructions done in the time violence or war. The taxpayers money meant originally for development is use to pay for this carnage. This is one of the fundamental tales of woes tracking down Africa Development.

Nigerian Government spent millions in both Pound Sterling and Dollar to acquire ammunition to tackle Niger-Delta imbroglio including the kidnapping saga in the far east of Niger-Delta. Even now, Millions of Dollars are budgeted annually to rehab ex-militants in Obudu Cattle Ranch since the date amnesty was granted to all militants across the Nation. The real fact here is that the money engaged at the moment could have been deployed before now to develop the Human Capital in this Country. Now, part of this fund marked out for the rehab purpose is finding its way into other economies outside Nigerian territory as Per Diem and salary paid to expatriates for consultancy. Same could have been directed at reviving dead refineries or even complement ongoing power project at Ajaokuta Steel Company.

For 50years after independence, Nigeria chance to become an advanced economy was hindered by poor leadership and endemic Corruption. Today, the best Nigerian Football stars live abroad, Best Nigerian Musicians either live or invest abroad, and the Best Nigerian Surgeons live abroad, Best Nigerian Nurses and Doctors live abroad, Best

Nigerian Educationists live abroad and the count continues ad inifinitum.

Bill Clinton in his last visit as a serving President of the United States of America mentioned that one of the best brains leading the revolution in the information and computer technology is a Nigerian. He is no other than Professor Philip Emeagwali whose innovative ingenuity helped in reducing the physical size of a supercomputer while upgrading the speed of its algorithms performance. This marked the birth of laptop and portable computers. In yet another feat conducted an experiment that provided the harbinger for the birth of the internet. According the information on his website (www.philipemeagwali.com) CNN declared him as the father of the internet. He has accomplished other feats that are very relevant in the rapid evolution information and computer technologies.

This population of Nigerians in Diaspora generates so much money such that the revenue they generate on annual basis outside Nigeria for their host Countries is equivalent to total GDP of about five Africa Nations put together. Imagine what the total revenue of entire African Community in Diaspora generates annually for Europe, USA, Asia and Australia; it will somehow equal the GDP of entire Africa for 5years. This is exactly one of the fundamental reasons for African under-development.

Growth of GDP of National Economy: Gross Domestic Product is a major parameter in determining the economic viability and development potential of an economy. Many Africa Nations are way far behind in tackling this most sensitive index that engineers development or on the other way; put the Country on the right stride toward positive and sustainable development. The GDP of many Nations not just in Africa are very poor and at such the future is bleak before them. Several factors are really responsible to this setback including;

- Incessant occurrences of natural disaster like tsunami, flooding, storms, earthquake, landslide, wildfire, and etcetera.

- Low Intelligent Quotient, IQ of Nations

- Poor Leadership leading to bad governance

- Unfavourable global leadership policies and practices that hinders the chances of infrastructural development of many poor Nations. Many global policies are forged, influenced and driven by very rich people, Nations, institutions and multinational companies which may likely shop nothing much in terms of development for poor Nations of the World.

- Terrorism potential increases the level of insecurity in many countries of the World, and at such many multi-national companies, investors, rich businessmen and global policies tends to be out of favour with such Nation.

- Lack of Human Capital Development

- Lack of the capacity to retain and profitably engaged the available trained skillful labourers in the system.

- Lack of access to good health facility and poor budget on Medicare

- Expired Education curriculum design that do not capture the paradigm shift of the 21st Century reality. In Africa, education is still an exclusive preserve of the rich. The poor consisting the greater percentages of the population are either idles without jobs or get involve in subsistent agricultural production. Worst is that most of the farmers do not access the government credit facility or grant to enable a large scale production at the end of the day.

- Hunger, malnutrition and food insecurity

- Systemic marginalization of the poor that constitute the larger percentage of the population in public debates, opinions and representation in both governance and at the government apex. This makes it even harder for the poor to escape clause of poverty tagging behind them daily.

- Misplacement of National budget priority to favour large budget allocation in development of the Military Might, large budget allocation for bailout to upsize Corporate gains that hike the margins of macro-economic performance but without a corresponding intrinsic value in the standard of living of the poor people. This increases the crisis of poverty at the downstream of the economy and reduces the chances of development and growth of the GDP.

- Structural Adjustment Program policies of the World Bank and International Monetary Fund, IMF that heap strategic advantages for the economically and politically advanced Nations of the World and against the slim chance for survival of many developing Nations. Such widening the gap of inequity and inequality of entities across the globe.

- Etc

What is perceived as the greatest gospel of globalization from all logical indication against this background is unfair advantage that the very Wealthy People or Nations enjoy at the moment while the rest of the World languishes in miserable poverty. World Bank and IMF encourages the poor Nations to compete among themselves and among the most advanced economies of the World in technology, resources and logistics capital development, Human Capital supply in provision of cheap labour and cheap raw materials for production. This is outright creation of profound imbalance in the global economic system.

Growth of National GDP of several poor Nations suffers in the pursuit of these Draconian policies and in the long run only managed to favour macroeconomic peak performance but without actually confronting the holocaust of poverty ravaging the masses at the lower cadre of the survival scale. This is a REALITY that the poor Nations of Africa must prepare to challenge if the chase for a better future must end on a solid note.

Regional Development:
We cannot grow the economy of the African region so long our LEADERS remain bedmates to Western Economic Buccaneers or to their representatives or institutions. African and other developing societies need to think for themselves considering their organic content, context and reality. We can begin to make visible progress the moment we begin to think right out of own intuition and instinctive value paradigm.

Yes! You can think global but you need to act locally to grow the business and revenue of the region. We need to cultivate our crops, process it and take patent over it. We can earn intellectual property revenue from abroad. We can think for ourselves in as developing nation. Advanced economies have grown in their economy, politics and social fashions, but are yet to grow in aptitude, attitude and amplitude to extend help to a growing economy without attaching traps.

Most aids to developing Nations comes in the baggage of quagmire woes as policies, this cannot help anyone indeed. Each region can actually work out a formula to go off debts and not trade the destiny of their offspring in advance to secure a short-term solution. Considering how much that has looted from Nigeria economy since independence, one can see without the aid of prophecy that the creature of Egypt has long assumed a more sophisticated and deceitful apron to siphon our economy via our leadership consistent financial corruption. All the money ever stolen by our Leaders are stashed in foreign accounts. How can they stop now since there is no way to stop them from keep the loot abroad?
Let the international community take away their aids and return back all the money stashed away in their treasury, Africa will be better. It will spark a new beginning for Africa. It will encourage the take off infant industry. It will keep the conspiracy theory of the rich in the dustbin and inspire a new spirit in the people.

Global Participation

There is no one person without good intention for the World. What has stopped many good intentions from manifesting is influence of Leaders who are using their own loyalists as fuel to cook own food. Those who send loyalist abroad to train in suicide bombing camps can use the same money to build schools or even factories to get them profitably employed to earn a living with dignity and integrity.

How come the cabals of terrorist groups are not sending their own children first on a suicide bomb mission before others? They cannot stand the destruction of their own blood, but are ready to make toast of wine in the air when others give up their life to keep them going and actualizing their mission. The ultra rich are always found to do one business anywhere in the World. That business is using follow humans as firewood fuel to cook their own food. They make more money to buy over your conscience and gradually brainwash you to believe that the other man is a big threat whereas they are the biggest threat.

Every people anywhere in the world can live side by side no matter their religion, race, colour, language or political bias without these breed of humans, and make useful contribution to the society.
There is nothing that makes an American superior over the man from Iraq; there is nothing that makes a Muslim superior over the other who is a Hindu or a Christian. All people are equal before the Maker and that is why all men breathe Oxygen to propagate existence.

The Creature: Unveiling The Revolution

References:

1. Ritchie, Felix – The Income Edge – The Revolution, 2010 Amazon Stores Worldwide.

2. Ritchie, Felix – Sagacity of Womanhood, 2011. Amazon Stores Worldwide & Barnes & Nobles

3. Ritchie, Felix – The 7th Dimension: Apocalypse of Wealth, 2011, USA. Amazon Stores Worldwide.

4. Donald Trump & Robert Kiyosaki – Why We Want You To Be Rich

5. Onwukwe, Jay – Wealth Secrets You must Before40, 2008

6. Kiyosaki, Kiyosaki – The Conspiracy of the Rich

7. Bangwell, kingsley - Emerging leaders, 2006/7 unpublished

8. Mensa, Otabil – Buy the Future

9. Robert, E. Kelley – How To Be a Star at Work, 1998,1999

10. De Bono, Edward. – Lateral Thinking: Creativity Step by Step. NY Harper & Row, 1990.

ABOUT THE BOOK:

The Creature from the Egyptian Pyramid shares Ritchie Felix insights and foresights about the global financial conundrum that has stripped the world of more than 10 million jobs, wiped away the middle class; and right now making the **Rich** move from **success** to **significance** in global finances while the rest of the world languishes in miserable poverty.

He cushions the blames of this turmoil on the lack of proper financial education in the world educational system which he dubbed the **"Knowledge Heist"** of the century. And without fear or compromise, he paralleled out remedies to help individuals and Nations to come out of this economic quagmire

Ritchie Felix words in this intellectual exposition unraveled the vast chasm separating the rich and the poor; and provided the congruence between supply and demand

The Creature: Unveiling The Revolution

consciousness in relative to individual perspectives of money or its prototype. It is a must read!

Ritchie Felix Profile:

- Former Science (Physics) Lecturer with Akwa-Ibom Polytechnic Aba Satellite Campus 2001 - 2003
- Assistant State Trainer for Abia/Imo State Youth Works Project Powered by British Council Nigeria in Collaboration Youngstars Development Initiatives captioned : " Top 12 " October 2007 – 2009
- Facilitator World Bank/Nokia Youth Training Workshop, 2007 & 2008
- Participated in Nigerian International e-Forum Powered by British Council & Youngstars Development Initiatives 2008
- Veteran of Nigerian Stakeholders Youth Forum (NSYF) caption: " Seven Points Agenda " of President Umar Musa Yar Adua
- Invited to speak on : " Challenge of Youth Poverty in Nigeria & Way Forward " in the National House of Assembly powered DFID, Young People Initiatives, USAID and National House Of Assembly 15th December, 2008
- Participated in NEPAD and Presidency as Special Development Envoy , December, 2008

- Resource Speaker at Assemblies of God National Youth Conference held in Abakiliki, August 2009
- e-Consultant for ICPD Policy Document (United Nation) on Youth & Reproductive Health, 2008/09
- DESPLAY Alumni: Democracy Series, Participation. Learning and Active Youth Season 4 powered National Endowment for Democracy, NED, Washington D.C in conjunction with Youngstars Development Initiatives 2008/09
- South-East Youth Delegate to: " Southern Youth Dialogue " Sponsored by International Republican Institute, IRI, Lagos , 2009
- One of the Four Nigerian Youth selected and participated in Democratic Internship at INEC Institute Federal Abuja; Sponsored by National Endowment for Democracy, NED, and Youngstars Development Initiatives, May, 2009
- Nigerian e-panelist at:" Global Pulse" March 23rd – 26th , 2010 powered by United States Government under President Barrack Obama in Collaboration with International Business Machine, IBM and USAIDs across the globe.
- Nigerian e-panelist at : " SERVICE JAM " October , 2010 Powered by International Business Machine, IBM, in Collaboration with united States Development Experts featured Ex- President George Bush as Guest on the Forum.
- Project Director Before40 Youth Empowerment Foundation 2010 till Date
- Invited by United State Goverment for Diplomatic Interaction with Ms Maria Oterio – USA Under Secretary of State for Democracy and Global Affairs at United States Consulate, Abuja March, 2011

- Facilitator Youth cyber Safety & Security Training Workshop powered By Youngstars Development Initiatives across the Federation April-May, 2011.

The Creature: Unveiling The Revolution

The Creature: Unveiling The Revolution

The Creature: Unveiling The Revolution

The Creature: Unveiling The Revolution

The Creature: Unveiling The Revolution

www.ingramcontent.com/pod-product-compliance
Lightning Source LLC
Chambersburg PA
CBHW051214170526
45166CB00005B/1892